ARNOLD PALMER'S
SUCCESS LESSONS

ARNOLD PALMER'S

SUCCESS LESSONS

*Wisdom on Golf, Business,
and Life from the King of Golf*

Previously titled *Mentored by the King*

BRAD BREWER

with Paul J. Batura

ZONDERVAN

Arnold Palmer's Success Lessons
Copyright © 2010, 2018 by Brad Brewer

Previously published as *Mentored by the King*

Requests for information should be addressed to:
Zondervan, 3900 Sparks Dr. SE, Grand Rapids, Michigan 49546

ISBN 978-0-310-35260-0 (softcover)

ISBN 978-0-310-35261-7 (ebook)

Library of Congress Cataloging-in-Publication Data

Brewer, Brad.
    Mentored by the king : Arnold Palmer's success lessons for golf, business, and
life / Brad Brewer with Paul J. Batura.
        p. cm.
    Includes bibliographical references (p.   ).
    ISBN 978-0-310-32661-8 (hardcover, jacketed)
    1. Golfers—Religious life. 2. Palmer, Arnold, 1929- 3. Golfing—Religious
aspects—Christianity. 4. Success—Religious aspects—Christianity. I. Batura, Paul J.
II. Title.
BV4596.G64B74 2010
158.1—dc22   2010039779

Published in association with the literary agency of Wolgemuth & Associates, Inc.

Cover design: Curt Diepenhorst
Cover photography: © Hulton-Deutsch Collection/Corbis via Getty Images®
Interior design: Sherri L. Hoffman

First printing January 2018 / Printed in the United States of America

This book is dedicated to my children—
Kenna, Carli, Tori, and Bradley.
Inspired with you in my thoughts,
I share what I was so privileged to experience
from a great mentor.

CONTENTS

PART 4
Heroes in Action

PART 5
A True Champion's Attitude Is Gratitude

On the Tee Box with Arnold Palmer

EVERY NOW AND AGAIN, a special sports figure emerges. Initially he appears rather ordinary, just another fresh face with raw skills and a healthy dose of persistence. A modicum of success follows. The performance captures our attention and piques our collective interest. Over the course of a career, this rare athlete rises, sometimes slowly, sometimes not, moving from prospect to professional, then to star—and finally to legend. It's only after several seasons of testing that he earns our genuine affection, commitment, and loyalty.

You see, we come to love a legend not just because of what he's done or won but because of the kind of man he's become and *how* he climbed that ladder of success. Everyone loves a winner on the field, but we especially admire those who are genuinely successful off the field as well.

"Character is like a tree and reputation like its shadow," Abraham Lincoln once said. "The shadow is what we think of it; the tree is the real thing."[1] My mentor and the subject of this project, golfing legend and elder statesman of the game Arnold Palmer, was one such man. And Arnold Daniel Palmer, a gentleman in the truest sense of the word, *was* the real thing.

There have been several wonderful books written about this golfing great. What makes this one unique? Well, for more than a quarter century, I had the pleasure of knowing and observing him as an employer, business partner, teacher, competitor, father, grandfather, philanthropist, global celebrity, and friend. I was a member of his entourage, walking the fairways from Augusta to St. Andrews, flying miles high with him in his private jet, and serving as the chief executive of his Arnold Palmer Golf Academies. As an intimate member of the Palmer team, it was my responsibility to develop and implement the school's curricula, open new locations, and even train the instructors hired to teach new students in the "Arnold Palmer" style of the game. I didn't just know how Arnold Palmer acted; I knew how he thought. I was familiar with what mattered most to him: his family and friends and his love of golf and its rich traditions. And I don't believe I've ever seen a man with a better work ethic or a more simplified and measured perspective of the game.

> *You go to the office and do your job. And you do it with a strong work ethic. If you win, you win. And if you lose, it's part of your job.*[2]

ARNOLD PALMER

Since our introduction in 1984, Arnold and I shared a marvelous teacher-student relationship. His mentorship helped me improve my game, but the truth is that he taught me much more than how to play great golf. By watching him navigate both the professional and the personal arenas of life, I have become a more effective coach and successful businessman who is rooted deeply in family and traditions. By his gracious and generous penchant for hospitality, he taught me lessons that almost seem at odds with the world: a busy person always has time for others, and nobody is more important than the next.

Anytime a writer sets out to capture the dynamics of a person, he runs the risk of lionizing his subject. Allow me to be clear. Like everyone else, Arnold was a mere mortal, an admirable but imperfect man. He was clearly driven, a perfectionist who probably struggled from time to time balancing his professional life. At times he was known to lose perspective, to become consumed by the challenge before him. But who among us doesn't have faults? To be sure, Mr. Palmer was no saint, but having spent twenty-five years with him, I'm moved to share the nuggets of wisdom I collected while watching him work. You may have spent countless weekends watching him from afar, mostly through television broadcasts and by reading the sports pages of your local newspaper. Some of you have met him in person, whether at a golf course, an airport, or maybe a restaurant. "Arnie's Army" is legendary and a force that cannot be ignored. Once, when asked to what he attributed his strong and loyal fan base, Arnold just smiled and replied in his characteristically succinct manner, "I got to know my fans, and they got to know me."[3]

It's my hope that as you read this book, you'll get to know him too. It's also my desire that you'll glean some very personal and practical life lessons from his long, storied, and fascinating life. Some are clear and obvious, getting "back to basics." Others might require more thoughtful consideration. In the following pages, you'll learn about Mr. Palmer's perspective on the power of dreams, the benefit of risks, and the importance of patience and persistence. You'll read how top golfers describe in their own words the lessons Arnold Palmer taught them — golfers such as Dicky Pride, Ian Baker-Finch, Peter Jacobsen, and Jack Nicklaus. And, of course, more than anyone else, you'll hear from Arnold Palmer himself: Behind-the-scenes stories. Never-before-published conversations that provide insights into the man people call "the King of golf." His thoughts culled over a lifetime about how he approached golf, business, and life so that you too can take further steps toward success.

What follows is my attempt to examine some wide-ranging lessons from a life well lived. It's my hope that these accounts will become as much a source of inspiration and guidance for you as they have been for me. I have been the beneficiary of many great and wonderful privileges, but none more so than the pleasure of being mentored by the King.

PART 1

LIFE-CHANGING LESSONS ARE OFTEN "DECEPTIVELY SIMPLE"

Golf is deceptively simple, endlessly complicated.
It frustrates the intellect and satisfies the soul.
The greatest game that mankind ever created.

ARNOLD PALMER

THE BEST THINGS IN LIFE are often simple on the surface but quite complex underneath. Think about it: the laugh and giggle of a child, the smell of a rose, the sight of a sunset along the surf or coast. Taken as a single snapshot, each of these joys is savored but rarely studied. Rare is the parent who considers the intricate and miraculous neurological system that cultivates and produces a laugh — or who really knows why a flower is so fragrant — or why a sky at twilight produces colors that even the world's best artist couldn't replicate.

So it goes with the great game of golf. On the surface, it strikes the casual observer as such an easy game. A club and a ball and some grass in between. What could possibly be so difficult?

But look beneath the surface and you'll soon begin to see what Arnold Palmer has been preaching about his entire life. Golf, though just a sport, has a streak of mystery to it. What you see is not all there is.

Remember Your Roots

ARNOLD PALMER'S OFFICE IS a choked-down lob wedge away from his residence and sits directly across the road from the Latrobe Country Club in Pennsylvania's leafy-green Laurel Highlands. Situated just east of the old steel mills of Pittsburgh, it seems an unlikely headquarters for the world's most accomplished and famous golfer. A man of means and influence, Palmer could have chosen to live anywhere, but there's no place he would rather call home than right here.

At eighty-one years old, the white-haired legend has traveled, played, and won titles and championships around the world. He's been a friend to presidents and heads of state, and you would be hard-pressed to find any award in sports or business that he was eligible for but hasn't yet received. In spite of all this, however, the trappings of celebrity haven't fazed or changed him. He still keeps his circle of friends small—all trusted people with whom he goes back decades. It's true that success has brought him fame and fortune, access and opportunity, but after every trip to victory or honor, all roads continue to bring him home, back to where it all began, back to the lush green hills of Latrobe, Pennsylvania.

EARLY BEGINNINGS

Arnold Palmer was born here just a few weeks prior to the great stock market crash on a late summer day, September 10, 1929. His parents, Doris and Milfred "Deacon" Palmer, lived beside the sixth tee of the Latrobe Country Club, in a small and simple but cozy house. So young Arnie has never been far from the game, nor has the game ever been very far from him. He still remembers leaning against a tree in that green backyard, a holster hugging his hip, and aiming his toy cap gun at a sand ditch in the distance. It was Ladies Day at the club. Even back then, you can be sure he hit the target.

His father, affectionately nicknamed Deacon, was the club's head groundskeeper and later golf pro and course superintendent. The elder Palmer's tenure at Latrobe stretched a remarkable span of fifty-five years, running until his death in 1976. Throughout his long run, Deacon had a knack for keeping things sharp and crisp, but the greatest testimony of his work was to be found in the form and success of his son.

"My psychologist was my father," Arnold once mused, "and he never went to college." Of course, his dad offered more than just advice. He first gave him clubs, an old cut-down set, at the tender age of four. There is nothing to suggest the boy was a prodigy, but he began to swing early and swing often. By all accounts, he was good, a natural talent. By the age of eleven, he was caddying. And playing. And watching. And learning and asking questions. By the time he left on September 7, 1947,[1] for Wake Forest University on a golf scholarship, Arnold had held nearly every job a kid could hold at Latrobe. Deacon's parting words were characteristically simple and straightforward: "Be tough, boy. Go out and play ... play your own game. If you start listening to other people's [advice], I have a job pushing a lawn mower here ... you can come back and do that."[2]

LOOKING BACK
When Arnold looks out the windows of his house or office or walks the course at Latrobe, he can't help but remember the

times he spent on the greens with his father. On the occasion of his eightieth birthday, he spent a day with a reporter from *USA Today*. His memory was razor sharp, right down to recalling the exact spot of a lesson borne of a fallen oak tree. Pointing to its location, a picturesque slice of earth on the edge of a green hill, Palmer began to tell the story:

> The trunk was rotten—I'll never forget this. A bunch of honeybees had moved in. Have you ever seen a honeycomb? Well, this one was full of honey. I mean, absolutely like that! [He spread his great hands like an exaggerating fisherman.] And my dad says, "Now, Arnie, we're going to take this honey home and give it to your mother, and we're going to eat it." But he says, "We've got to get two five-pound bags of sugar. When we take the honey out, we're going to put those two bags of sugar right there, so the bees can have their food...." I was about seven or eight years old.

To know Arnold Palmer is to know a man who took his late father's lesson of that memorable day to heart. He is a man who gives back, a generous soul eager and inclined to give away far more than he receives. As the reporter who walked the course with him on that day concluded, by his advice and actions with those bees seven decades ago, Deacon Palmer taught his son a simple but wonderfully practical lesson: "When you take the honey out, put some sugar back in."[3]

HAPPY TO BE HOME

Happy is the person, a wise man once wrote, who still loves as an adult something he loved in childhood; time has not torn him in two. The same might be said of my good friend. Sitting and talking with Arnold Palmer in his home office, watching him swivel and rock gingerly in the tall chair behind an eight-foot-long antique wooden desk, is to watch a man very much at peace with himself and comfortable with the many loves of his life. It is an unusual thing, isn't it, to have accomplished so much, to have gone so far, and yet to return and be content spending the twilight of your career only steps from where you were born. Where others might be struck with wanderlust, thinking the next stop of the journey will be better than the last, Palmer is satisfied to stay close to home.

Visit Arnold Palmer's hometown and talk with its residents, and it quickly becomes clear that the local boy who made good set down roots that ran deep. He watered them daily and invested heartily in his hometown friends and neighbors. The legend looks beyond just the geographical boundaries, however, when assessing the tug toward home. "Your hometown is not where you're from," he's said. "It's who you are."[4] Reporters regularly ask why he stays and continues to invest not only his time but his resources in the community. "I've done a lot of things and I will always have some connection here in Latrobe, or Pittsburgh, if you wish. I love this area. If the good Lord is willing, I'll be around here for a while to enjoy it some more."[5] As Arnold Palmer enters his ninth decade of life, his prayers have been answered. This favorite son of Latrobe, Pennsylvania, is happy to be home.

And home is where he is happiest of all.

You Are What You Think

THE PLAQUE HAS HUNG on Arnold's office wall for years, but to the best of his memory, he doesn't recall when he received it or from whom. Until recently, he didn't even know who authored the beautifully engraved inspirational verses. Nevertheless, it's clear Arnold Palmer has taken them to heart.

The inscription is titled "The Man Who Thinks He Can,"[1] and it was written by a little-known poet from the late nineteenth and early twentieth centuries by the name of Walter D. Wintle. The verses, with minor variations, have been widely quoted for years by entrepreneurs such as insurance magnate Napoleon Hill and automaker Henry Ford. Renowned preachers Norman Vincent Peale and Robert Schuller have considered the poem — next to the Bible — to be foundational reading. The words hang in locker rooms all across America. The poem has been a favorite of at least two football coaching legends, Vince Lombardi and Penn State's iron horse, Joe Paterno. For Arnold Palmer, the thoughts in this poem have given rise to his approach to life, whether on the golf course, in the boardroom, or at his kitchen table. Here is Walter Wintle's poem:

The Man Who Thinks He Can

If you think you are beaten, you are;
If you think you dare not, you don't.
If you'd like to win, but you think you can't,

It's almost certain you won't.
If you think you'll lose, you've lost;
For out in the world you'll find
Success begins with a fellow's will;
It's all in the state of mind.

If you think you are outclassed, you are;
You've got to think high to rise.
You've got to be sure of yourself before
You can ever win a prize.
Life's battles don't always go
To the stronger or faster man;
But sooner or later the man who wins
Is the man who thinks he can.

Whether you think you can or can't, you are probably right.
AUTOMAKER HENRY FORD

My time with Arnold Palmer has made clear many things, but none more so than the fact that he embodies a quiet sense of confidence and strength. He lives and breathes these words. Through the years, there may have been stronger or longer hitters, better chippers, or more consistent putters on the PGA Tour, and in a career that stretched over four decades, others might have had a better year now and again. But year in and year out, Palmer always believed he was capable of coming out on top in each and every tournament he entered. "I've always made a total effort, even when the odds seemed entirely against me," he's said. "I never quit trying; I never felt that I didn't have a chance to win."[2]

Still, he never was, nor is, a braggart. If confidence is courage at ease, this Pennsylvania native has always seemed to exude a beautiful sense of serenity, both on and off the course. Ask him how he does it, and he'd suggest the qualities are borne of preparation, hard work, repetition, and a firm belief in having fun playing aggressively to win. Sounds pretty simple, but how did he get there? Is a man born a confident star? Is there really such a thing as a self-made man? Over the years, in different venues and in different forms, I've asked him those very questions.

"Well, I suppose you could say that I became motivated by reading these words [Wintle's] almost daily," he replied, "and they began to resonate with my thoughts that I can really do whatever I put my mind to, whether it's with my golfing aspirations or anything else for that matter."[3]

> *Ability is what you're capable of doing. Motivation determines what you do. Attitude determines how well you do it.*
>
> LOU HOLTZ

Though he was speaking about the pursuit of excellence in golf, his philosophy translates into every area of life. "Ninety-five percent of the game is from the shoulders upwards," he offered on one occasion.[4] He's right. People laughed when the legendary Yogi Berra observed that "baseball is 90 percent mental; the other half is physical."[5] Yogi might have a problem with math, but he understands what Arnold Palmer preaches, and he's aware how important it is to believe in yourself. If you're going to succeed, if you're going to accomplish great things, you have to be in the right frame of mind—and you can't start soon enough. As he does on a regular basis, Arnold insists you must find the right message that inspires you to take action *today* toward your worthy ideal of *tomorrow*.

A COMMITTED STATE OF MIND

The Leadville Trail 100 Ultramarathon, also called "The Race Across the Sky," is a remarkable endurance running event held every summer in the mountains of western Colorado. Fewer than half of the runners who enter every year actually finish the 100-mile trek within the thirty-hour time limit. The course is brutal. Throughout the ordeal, runners climb and descend a total of 15,600 feet from a minimum elevation of 9,200 feet to a maximum of 12,620. For flatlanders, that's some rarified air, to be sure!

The race's founder, Ken Chlouber, is a beloved character, known as much for his affinity for endurance racing as he is for his popular annual pep talks before the competition. Gathering the entrants in the predawn dark each year, Chlouber uses a style that is both humorous and pointed. "You're all crazy!" he tells entrants. "We'll tell you when to start and we'll tell you when to stop. In between, don't think, just keep running." Those gathered laugh nervously, but soon Ken settles in for the punch line. "You're better than you think you are," he hollers. "You can do more than you think you can."

Most of us perform beneath our level of energy.[6]
ARCHBISHOP FULTON J. SHEEN,
ROMAN CATHOLIC APOLOGIST

Arthur Gordon, an author and former editor of *Guideposts* magazine, once told the story of a British mountain climber. The adventurer would regularly find himself in positions where he couldn't go back down, so steep and dangerous was the climb. But he added that every now and again, he would purposely put himself in danger. Why? How did he get himself out of the predicament? "When there's nowhere to go but up," he offered, "you jolly well go up."[7]

THE POWER OF REPETITION

Radio commentator Paul Harvey used to say, somewhat jokingly, "Repetition is effective. Repetition is effective. Repetition is effective."[8] Golfer Gary Player has been linked with similar advice, noting that the more a person practices, the "luckier" they seem to get. Arnold Palmer would agree that when it comes to learning a new skill or perfecting an old one, daily repetition is the greatest secret of all. Whether in golf or any other pursuit, beginning is half done.

Repetition penetrates even the dullest of minds.[9]

LEGENDARY GOLF INSTRUCTOR
DAVID LEADBETTER

But while "beginning" and "doing" will take you places, it should go without saying that you need to know where you want to land. I once heard about a famous sculptor who chiseled stone for days. "What are you making?" someone finally asked him. "I really don't know," he replied. "I haven't seen the plans."[10]

We must visualize our goal. Flexibility is crucial, but planning is critical. Discipline is not always doing the same thing the same way; sometimes it's finding a different way to arrive at the same result. Through the process of hearing affirming words and forming inspiring thoughts, over and over again, you begin to program the positive course that makes you feel that you can do what you set out to accomplish. You begin to believe that God has a plan for your life and that he really does care about the details, however small some of them may seem to others.

A word of warning: Negative and cynical thinking might

come so naturally that you're hardly even aware of just how downbeat your thoughts have become. I'd encourage you to try a little exercise. When something happens, whether expected or unexpected, examine your initial reaction. Do you immediately think the worst? Maybe it's time for some adjustments. Instead of saying, "I hope," why not substitute "I will"? Or rather than lamenting, "It's a big problem," how about, "It's a big opportunity"? One of my favorite exercises comes from Dr. Norman Vincent Peale, whose legendary simplicity was part of his genius. "Take the 't' off the 'can't,'" he'd say.[11] And marvelous things will happen.

Arnold Palmer is a man who has practiced that principle his whole life, because he's a man who believes that "whether you think you can or can't, you are probably right."

Tell Me That I Am Ready

LATE ONE EVENING, I was taking a few swings on the back of the driving range at Bay Hill, a private teeing ground designated for Academy lessons and Tour professional members. The facility is housed inside Arnold Palmer's Orlando resort, a short drive from our family's home. As I reached down to set up my next ball, Mr. Palmer drove up in a golf cart, his beloved golden retriever, Prince, sitting beside him. We greeted one another warmly. The "King" then proceeded to throw down his personal shag bag, which was filled with new monogrammed Callaway golf balls.

Even after all these years, it's still fun to share a driving range with a star. Our games might be a mile apart, but to stand side by side with a legend who's doing the same thing you are, although admittedly much better, is still a rare and wonderful treat. Arnold began his practice session by striking a few eight irons to a target green 150 yards away. He was as pure and accurate as if he were driving a car rather than a ball. Thinking ahead to a seminar I was scheduled to conduct for a group of PGA professionals, I couldn't help but seize the opportunity to ask a few questions.

"Mr. Palmer," I began, "in your mind, what's the most important thing that I can do in coaching a good player?"

He answered as quickly as if he had been waiting for me to

ask that particular question his entire life. "Tell me how good I am and that I'm ready to win," he said.

CULTIVATING A CONFIDENT STATE OF MIND

Having coached competitive golfers for years, I can attest to the effectiveness of Palmer's simple wisdom. NBA hall-of-famer Michael Jordan was arguably the world's greatest basketball player, but his career climb wasn't straight up. He was infamously cut from his high school team, but he later cited that experience as a turning point, a time when he learned the importance of setting goals and believing they were attainable. "Don't live down to expectations," Jordan has counseled. "You have to expect things of yourself before you can do them."[1]

Some might be concerned this principle feeds a spirit of arrogance and conceit. And if you're not careful, it could. Retired heavyweight boxing champion Muhammad Ali had a reputation for making sure everyone knew he considered himself the best prizefighter who ever lived. In a candid moment, Ali once admitted, "I figure that if I said it enough, I would convince the world that I really was the greatest."[2] But with an Olympic gold medal and a career record of sixty-one wins and five losses, Ali's own response to the charge rings true: "It's not bragging if you can back it up."[3]

Arnold Palmer doesn't suffer from the malady of self-bravado. He's confident but not cocky. And he doesn't just believe in himself; he believes in his plan, in his preparation, and in his ability to execute on demand. I've seen the power and impact of instilling this strong spirit of self-confidence in an athlete.

The will to win means nothing without the will to prepare.[4]
WORLD-CLASS TANZANIAN MARATHONER
JUMA IKANGAA

A short time ago, in fact, I was given the opportunity to help a young and struggling PGA Tour professional. His dramatic and successful turnaround mid-season was nothing short of remarkable.

A FORTUNATE MEETING

It was June of 1997, and my wife, Wanda, and I were invited to a cocktail party. While there, we were introduced to a young Australian Tour professional named Bradley Hughes and had a few moments to chat about his career and some of our mutual acquaintances. He was quite interested in my friendship and experiences with Arnold Palmer, and, as always, I was happy to engage him in a conversation about a man we both greatly admired. We promised to talk again but parted company without any set plans to meet.

Two weeks later I received a call from Bradley's wife, Laura, who had been thinking about our visit and asked to set up a meeting. She wanted to talk about contracting with me to give her husband some help with his game. Since there was a sense of urgency in her voice, I didn't waste any time. I cleared the calendar, and the very next day the three of us sat down together to discuss Bradley's current position on the PGA Tour and what areas of his game he believed were holding him back.

It's my custom with any student to get a firsthand look at their game before offering any substantive advice. It's as impossible to teach golf by just talking as it is to write out directions on how to tie a necktie. We went out on the course, where I watched him strike several shots in a practice situation. Frankly, I was stunned. Despite his slump, I quickly concluded that this man had one of the best golf swings I had ever seen! So what was the problem? Bradley acknowledged a weakness and inconsistency with his putting. He was also struggling with his short irons. I understood what his PGA Tour stats indicated: he was a top-ten ball striker (i.e., someone with a masterful talent to control the trajectory, distance, and direction of a shot) on the Tour, but he continued to fall short of the top 125 on the money list over the past three years. As I delved into the scoring zone shots, we noticed a glaring need for improvement of Bradley's chipping and putting performance.

Fortunately, "Hugo," as he's known on the Tour, was the ideal student. He had all the qualities a golf instructor loves to have in a client: he was a realist; he was hungry, eager, and motivated; and he had a teachable spirit. We immediately went to work on his putting, and at the end of that very same day, Hugo and I sat down to talk.

"I know that you're extremely concerned that it's halfway through the season," I told him, "and you're currently way below the top 125 on the money list. I also know you're concerned about losing your coveted PGA Tour card and being forced to return to Tour School next year."

He nodded, knowing full well that I was aware of the pressure he was under.

"Hugo, did you know in any one given year, 80 percent of the money made on tour by a player is on average won within seven weeks?" I said, referring to a classic piece of Palmer wisdom. "These are the hot weeks when it all seems to click."

His eyes brightened and he leaned forward, keenly interested and encouraged by this new perspective.

"Your golf swing is fundamentally sound, and, with good practice on the chipping and putting and a more relaxed attitude about your current position on the money list, I believe you'll begin performing to the level of your great talent. But don't force it. Just let it happen."

Three weeks later, Bradley finished second at the PGA Tours FedEx in Memphis, and he called me excitedly to say, "I guess that is the first of the seven for this year!"

Bradley Hughes finished that year with more than enough winnings to keep his PGA Tour card, and he stopped his four-year cycle of returning to the PGA Qualifying School (also known as Q-school).[5] More importantly, he began once again to believe in himself and in his existing abilities by employing some of Arnold Palmer's classic and fundamental wisdom. Like Palmer had taught me to do, I had evaluated Hugo and could honestly tell him that I believed he was ready to win. Fortunately, Hugo was ready to listen.

FOCUS ON YOUR STRENGTHS

Best-selling author and management guru Ken Blanchard has made a career encouraging others to seize and capitalize on the positive aspect of their gifts and talents. In his classic book *The One Minute Manager*, Ken urged bosses to "catch people doing things right."[6] Blanchard knows how to motivate. We all need to be affirmed, and acknowledging someone's talents is a great way to do it. The Gallup organization recently published a series of development-oriented books centered on this concept of accentuating the good. *StrengthsFinder 2.0* is based on an amazingly simple principle: Most people spend so much time trying to improve their weaknesses that they ignore the opportunity to develop their strengths and unique talents.[7] Instead of focusing on the negative, spend time developing and nurturing your areas of natural giftedness.

Hide not your talents. They for use were made. What's a sundial in the shade?

BENJAMIN FRANKLIN

"Tell me how good I am." We all need to give and receive this type of encouragement in our lives, but how do we do it? Begin by taking inventory of the people around you. What are they saying to you? Are they supporting your dreams and goals? Or are they always negative, inclined to see a glass half empty instead of half full? These are the ones who suck joy from life, who seem to enjoy robbing you of hope and making you as miserable as they might very well be themselves. It's critically important to stave off feelings of inadequacy and self-doubt. Find someone who can and who will tell you how good you really are today and what you can become tomorrow.

> *The dream never stops, just the dreamer. The song never stops, just the singer.*[8]

> THE REVEREND H. B. LONDON

THE SECRET TO A GREAT PERFORMANCE

Hugo's success story teaches us something else: when we calm things down, we can actually speed up and more quickly accomplish our goals. When Bradley quit worrying about his past performance and realized he had plenty of time to right his wayward ship, he put things into perspective, calmed his spirit, and began performing at the level of his potential.

Jim Loehr is a sports psychologist and author of the bestselling book *The New Toughness Training for Sports*. He too subscribes to the Arnold Palmer philosophy of athletic performance. "Nobody plays better when feeling the pressure," he wrote. "Great performers learn how to survive and then thrive in the pressure cooker by depressurizing themselves in a pressure situation."[9] When athletes like Arnold Palmer and Bradley Hughes are able to deal adequately with stress, they're far more likely to remain focused on the process of execution instead of becoming emotionally caught up with overthinking the significance of the moment.

We've all heard that we have to learn from our mistakes, but I think it's more important to learn from successes. If you learn only from your mistakes, you are inclined to learn only errors.[10]

NORMAN VINCENT PEALE

We'll revisit this important topic of managing pressure versus pressure managing us in later chapters. In the meantime, it's important to be aware of how easy it is to get emotionally wrapped up over negative "stuff." Agonizing over past failures or fearing the future will drain us of our self-confidence faster than a drop of water evaporates off my car's hood in the Florida summer heat. This "stuff" begins to cloud our better judgment and detract from our ability to know who we are, what skills we possess, and what it is that we truly desire to accomplish. For this very reason, don't ever underestimate the value of someone who can tell you how good you are and that you are ready to win!

Simplify the Complex

SHOULD YOU EVER CROSS PATHS with any of my students from the past twenty years, they will undoubtedly remember my recitation of a favorite Arnold Palmer quote:

> Golf is deceptively simple and endlessly complicated. A child can play it well and a grown man can never master it. Any single round of it is full of unexpected triumphs and perfect shots that end in disaster. It is almost a science, yet it is a puzzle without an answer. It is gratifying and tantalizing, precise and unpredictable; it requires complete concentration and total relaxation. It satisfies the soul and frustrates the intellect. It is at the same time rewarding and maddening — and it is without doubt the greatest game mankind has ever invented.[1]

That brilliantly sums up everything that the great and beautiful game of golf is *and* can be. I've thought about these words for years, and I've arrived at a simple conclusion: I'm drawn to Mr. Palmer's perspective for no other reason than this — he is right!

Just today, for example, I was preparing for the Florida Open at the Interlachen Country Club, a picturesque course in Winter Park, Florida, a suburb of Orlando. Practicing on the par three, number eight hole, playing 218 yards, I hit my purest three iron of the day. It felt deceptively simple. The ball coming off the center of the club face sent a positive feeling from head to toe. Landing three feet to the right of the cup, it took an excessively large bounce and came to rest just off the green, settling on the short side of the pin. I surveyed the lie and concluded that my chances of an up-and-down—getting it "up" onto the green and "down" into the hole—were nearly impossible. I was naturally frustrated, especially given that it was my finest strike of the day.

The hits just kept coming. I approached my next shot and swung softly, but the ball landed twelve feet from the hole. Fortunately, positive thinkers know full well that failure is never final, and the great equalizer came on the next shot. It was sweet justice as I "holed" the long putt and gained back the satisfaction of parring an extremely challenging hole.

Arnold Palmer is right. Even a committed player of the game will quickly discover, within a ten-minute journey on a par-three hole, that the game of golf is deceptively simple and endlessly complicated.

BACK-TO-THE-BASICS SIMPLICITY

Given how foundational Palmer's philosophy of simplifying complexity has been to me, I've naturally been curious about how and where it originated. During a visit to his Latrobe office, I decided to ask.

"What has helped you keep your thoughts so deceptively simple about such complex things?" I asked.

Arnold leaned back in his chair, rubbed his chin, and gazed out the window, his eyes brightening, his gaze settling on the distant course.

"It was the way my father and mother raised me," he began. "My dad taught me how to play, and he would keep it to the basic fundamentals, like a good grip, steady head, and the need to just hit it hard! That was fun for me, and it gave me great satisfaction to strike the ball this way when I was a young man. As I progressed during my career, if I ever felt like I was out of sorts, I would just go back to these simple thoughts, and I would find that 'solid ball-striking' that leads to winning golf tournaments again.

"But I have seen many fellow competitors get twisted into knots," he continued, "trying new things and searching for that magical swing, though to no avail. In fact, some unfortunate fellows just over-thought themselves right off the Tour and out of competitive golf. I tried to keep all of my energy focused on my goal of winning every tournament that I entered. My thought was to create and execute good shots, one at a time. Not perfect swings, but keeping it simple with basic fundamentals that produced the good golf shots that proved to serve me well."

BREAKING BAD HABITS

As a pro whose responsibility it is to "fix" the broken swings of my students, I find Palmer's "swing thoughts" refreshingly (though deceptively) simple. Mere mortals like us might easily discount them. After all, unlike Arnold Palmer or Tiger Woods or Annika Sorenstam, many of us didn't begin playing golf as a young boy or girl, or benefit from a parent or coach instilling good golfing habits back then. There's a tremendous advantage in learning these simple lessons at a young age, before faulty habits set in and negative thoughts become the norm. Fortunately, just because you didn't begin playing at age six doesn't mean that you can't reprogram your habits toward achieving what you want to accomplish.

If you've only picked up the game as an adult, take heart. The vast majority of players out there have done the very same thing.

Elevating your game begins with awareness that certain fundamentals are necessary to develop a repeatable shot pattern. This newly practiced paradigm will require conscious thought for a while, with several repetitions, before it becomes your newly formed habit. What I'm suggesting is nothing new, of course, but a return to the basic fundamentals of the game can be one of the most important things a golfer can do.

> *The secret of getting ahead is getting started. The secret of getting started is breaking your complex overwhelming tasks into small manageable tasks, and then starting on the first one.*
> MARK TWAIN

How long does it take to develop good golfing habits? Of course, every individual is unique, but scientists have studied the length of time the average person needs to reach a level of what they call "automaticity" for a particular skill, referring to the ability to do something without having to force it or struggle to break an old habit. (You might hear someone say they "don't even have to think" about what they're doing, but that's rarely the case in sports. Show me a golfer who doesn't think about his shots, and I'll show you a golfer who spends most of his time looking for errant balls.) Researchers have discovered that when it comes to forming a new habit, the length of time needed ranges from 18 to 254 days, but the average person takes approximately 66 days.[2] That might seem like a long time, but it's less than a summer, and, given that we're emphasizing *simplicity*, I've discovered that my average student can usually break faulty habits and form new ones in only a couple of weeks. Personally, I would strongly suggest finding a good certified LPGA or PGA teaching professional who can help you define your basics, simplify your thoughts, and have more fun.

At the root of Arnold Palmer's advocacy for simplicity is the fact that he's also well grounded in the moment. Despite his credentials in the Hall of Fame, he still remembers what it's like to be starting out in the game, and he understands that if you're going to do anything complicated well for a long period of time, you have to keep it simple, a paradox he is more philosophical about than most golfers. "One of the most fascinating things about golf," he has said, "is how it reflects the cycle of life. No matter what you shoot, the next day you have to go back to the first tee and begin all over again and make yourself into something."[3] It's this internal drive that keeps him playing into his eighties, always challenging the complex but never quite satisfied with his ability to keep things simple.

And so Mr. Palmer's lessons are simple, even though he knows that execution and accomplishment very often are not. Even the King himself is well aware of the limitations posed by golf's complexity. "If you are caught on a golf course during a storm and are afraid of lightning," Palmer once cracked, "hold up a one-iron. Not even God can hit a one-iron."[4]

> *My pitching philosophy is simple. You gotta keep the ball off the fat part of the bat.*[5]
>
> SATCHEL PAIGE, THE FIRST NEGRO LEAGUE
> BASEBALL PLAYER INDUCTED INTO THE
> NATIONAL BASEBALL HALL OF FAME

But I've discovered that Palmer's positive mental conditioning at an early age has allowed him to respond with a trust in his simple approach to the game. It's occurred to me that the mind is like a computer. When you have too many programs open at the same time, the computer's processor can cause the hard drive to lock up or crash. The same thing happens with our thinking. If you keep things simple and remain focused on what you want to accomplish, your mind and body can do a better job of communicating and achieving the desired golf shot, business decision, or personal goal.

The simpler the better!

Define Your Worthy Ideal

ON THE WALL AT Arnold Palmer's Bay Hill Club in Orlando, in the hallway leading up to the King's office, is a small plaque. It reads: "Golf is not a matter of life or death. It's much more important than that!"[1]

At an early age, Arnie aspired to be a champion golfer. In fact, he can't remember a day when he didn't want to play professionally. To fully appreciate and understand the motivations of a legend, it's necessary, I think, to understand more about his dreams, goals, and aspirations. I can't speak for every legend, but looking at the arc and trajectory of Arnold Palmer's career, he didn't just become a champion because he spent more time on the golf course than everyone else.

> *Champions aren't made in the gyms. Champions are made from something they have deep inside them—a desire, a dream, a vision.*[2]
>
> BOXING LEGEND MUHAMMAD ALI

So what *was* the big picture in the King's mind and when did it begin to form? Back in Arnie's office, I decided to ask him. "I'd like to share a quote with you from the Pittsburgh steel magnate Andrew Carnegie," I told him.

I could see that he was intrigued by the reference and perhaps even puzzled by how I was going to connect golf with the steel industry. But Arnold is very familiar with Andrew Carnegie since the man made his mark and fortune, albeit a few generations earlier, not far from Latrobe.

"Please, go right ahead," Arnold responded. "Fire away, Brad."

"An idea that's held in the mind, emphasized, feared, or revered begins to clothe itself in the most convenient and appropriate physical form that's available,"[3] I recited, quoting Carnegie.

At that point, Palmer was wading through the papers in front of him. "As I look at your life," I told him, "and I look at all your accomplishments, my question to you is that when you set out on your path of turning professional, going after this 'worthy ideal' of becoming the best golfer you could be, what were your dreams, what were your goals? Was it to be the number one player in the world?"

The question appeared to infuse him with energy. "Well," he began excitedly, "I suppose that you could say that my goals were to win golf tournaments. In those days the first thing that I thought about was *winning* tournaments. Back then, they didn't talk about the majors like they do today. In those days it was the Masters and the Open. A lot of people didn't even think about the British Open and, of course, the PGA. But I remember somebody saying, 'What are you going to do? Are you going to get really ready for the Masters or are you going to get really ready for the U.S. Open?' Personally, I felt that you just win tournaments. Winning the Masters or the Open isn't the only thing in the world. Every golf tournament you play in, as far as I was concerned, was a Masters or an Open or the PGA or British Open — and I played them like that. You're playing the same people in the same situation, and I wanted to win them as much as I wanted to win anything. That was my goal. That was my aim."

I leaned forward in my chair. "So your aim was to stay focused one step at a time?"

Mr. Palmer smiled. "Right. People asked, 'Why did you go to the British Open in 1960? What drove you to do that?' Well, the drive to be a great player was part of what drove me to the British Open, because I didn't feel like you could be a great player if you couldn't win internationally. So I had to go to the British Open. For the moment, I had a singular focus. The goal was just to win it one time; it wasn't a question of winning multiple British Opens. But I had to win it. Needless to say, I thoroughly enjoyed it. It was a real kick for me to win the British Open. The first time, when I lost by a shot to Kel Nagle, was also a kick; it was something that pleased me very much and drove me to keep going."

LOOKING BACK

"Success is the progressive realization of a worthy ideal," motivational speaker and author Earl Nightingale said.[4] A "worthy ideal" is not just another great idea; it's an idea that's better than all the rest. It's not just an idea that you like; it's something you love. It's the thing you would do anything to achieve, the thing you would give up almost everything else you possess in an effort to gain. The worthy ideal is also the thing you never give up pursuing regardless of how many times you fall down or fail trying.

Success is the progressive realization of a worthy ideal.
MOTIVATIONAL SPEAKER AND AUTHOR
EARL NIGHTINGALE

The typical journey toward greatness is laced with heartache and hardship. If they do fall, winners get up, dust themselves off, and grow from the experience. Victors don't lose the vision of the goal; the guiding vision is part of their heart and soul. Those most devoted to their worthy ideal would tell you they would rather fight to the death than consider giving up short of the finish line.

Inspired by his early string of successes, Arnold Palmer continued to steadily move closer to his worthy ideal of becoming the greatest golfer in the world. In some ways, this sounds obvious, but knowing where you want to end up before you embark on your journey is critical if you're going to have any chance of getting there. You'd be surprised how many people forget how important it is to map out a deliberate and detailed strategy— or even clearly state an objective. It's become a bit of a cliché, quoted in music and recent films, but "if you don't know where you're going, any road will take you there."[5] It sounds good, but it's just not so. Your destination will be determined by other forces. I'm more inclined to embrace the wisdom of Yogi Berra. "You've got to be very careful if you don't know where you're going," he once mused, "because you might not get there."

No Guarantees

Of course, even having the soundest plan and clearest vision doesn't mean you'll never take a wrong turn or two. A career as long as Palmer's saw its share of ups and downs. In the late 1960s, Arnold was given his first real test. Between September of 1968 and November of 1969, he failed to win a tournament. He made some adjustments and stormed back to claim $209,603 in winnings in 1971. But in 1972 he hit the skids again and went the entire year without a championship, acknowledging some of his struggles with declining eyesight. How did he respond?

In an interview at the end of 1972, the predictably philosophical Palmer said he was going to take some time off and recalibrate. "I won't play until I'm satisfied my game is good enough," he stated. "That may cause me to miss a few events, but that's better than going out there and building up frustration."[6]

Regarding his decision, he said, "I feel good about it — especially when I hear some of those people out there in the gallery. Those wonderful people ... they're the ones who keep pushing on. They walk with me on good days and on bad days, and they're always urging me on. They send me nice encouraging letters, playing tips, good luck charms, and all that. Why, I guess if I'd never won a purse out there, I'd still have to consider myself a rich man just to have them on my side."[7]

SET YOUR SIGHTS

When your picture of success is fixed in your mind, it becomes like the North Star to the sailor, providing a constant bearing by which to guide your efforts. All too often we play it safe; we fail to fully commit to the direction of our worthy ideal. There could be several reasons for this, the most common one being our fear of failure. We often try to explain away our reluctance to take a chance by repeating some version of the following: "If I commit to my dreams and fall short, then I'll be disappointed — maybe even devastated. I'll be terribly embarrassed if anyone finds out how pathetic I really am. It's better and safer to just wait and see what happens, and if I begin seeing that I could really do something, then I will reset my goals."

Does this — which might qualify as the "Underachiever's Creed" — sound familiar? The problem with this "wait and see" approach is that all too often we give up at the first sign of difficulty or disappointment, and it's impossible to benefit from the laws of momentum if you're standing or sitting still.

If you're really in love with an idea, you must do as Arnold Palmer did and commit yourself to making it happen. You have to live and breathe the dream. It sounds almost like a cliché, but it's true: great discoveries come only when the captain of the ship is willing to lose sight of the shore. You often have to take a chance and assume the risks that accompany the adventure. Robert F. Kennedy, a U.S. senator, attorney general, and civil rights activist, said, "Only those who dare to fail greatly can ever achieve greatly."

You don't need to have all the answers and you certainly don't need to possess all of the resources in order to capture the vision of your worthy ideal. But the ascent and career of Arnold Palmer should remind us that catching a clear glimpse of your goal is the best and only way to give your dream a chance to come true.

Always Give a Firm Handshake

IF YOU EVER HAVE the pleasure of shaking hands with the King, you'll never forget it. Given his reputation and larger-than-life personality, it probably wouldn't surprise you to learn that Arnold Palmer shakes hands with strength and purpose. In fact, Jerry Tarde, the chairman and editor-in-chief of *Golf Digest*, once humorously described shaking hands with Palmer for the first time by saying, "Those huge mitts swaddled mine like a sandwich made with a loaf of Wonder Bread."[1] That's well said!

"If you are going to shake someone's hand," Arnie once told me, "then grab a firm hold and look them in the eye. A man's handshake should be as good as his word. You can throw away all the contracts ever written by the best attorneys. Written contracts can all be broken. All my important deals were done with a handshake."

The most famous of those handshake contracts sealed a historic business relationship with Mark McCormack, a man Palmer had met and played golf against in college. After McCormack graduated from Yale Law School, he approached his friend with an idea to "brand" the legend and promised to make him wealthy in the process. In just the first two years, Palmer's endorsement deals jumped from $6,000 annually to $500,000.[2] Soon McCormack's venture exploded into a billion-dollar company, and the most powerful sports marketing company in the world, International Management Group, commonly referred to as IMG, soon gained worldwide fame.[3]

Palmer regularly states that his word is as strong as his handshake, and, as Jerry Tarde can verify, his handshake can crush walnuts and knuckles if you don't deliver the same amount of pressure in return.

RESEARCH BEHIND THE HANDSHAKE

Paul J. Zak, who is the director of the Center for Neuroeconomics Studies at Claremont Graduate University in Claremont, California, suggests there is some solid science to back up the emotional and professional benefits of handshaking. "Neuroscientists have shown that when we are trusted by a stranger, this engages the same brain systems as other kinds of social bonds," Zak wrote, "from friendship to the love of a parent for a child to the love of your spouse. These bonds are maintained through oxytocin, a simple brain chemical ancient in origin."[4] Zak found that the human brain "uses oxytocin to unconsciously assess if a person is trustworthy, using our memory of past encounters and all of our senses, including touch. If the stranger is a good match for other trustworthy people, the brain releases oxytocin, telling us it is safe to trust."[5]

I can feel the twinkle of his eye in his handshake.

HELEN KELLER

This simple belief in the tradition and value of the common handshake reveals much about the character of Arnold Palmer. Science notwithstanding, it's been my observation that Palmer possesses a keen sense of intuition, or what some might call a "sixth sense." By all accounts, Arnold is an excellent observer of people and has surrounded himself with quality individuals his entire career, something we'll discuss in a later chapter. But suffice it to say that so many of Arnold's associates have been with him for decades because he knows how to find people who possess a great work ethic and high integrity, qualities they also recognize in Palmer.

GET A GRIP

Speaking of Arnold Palmer's grip, I learned very early on just how strong his hands and forearms truly are. In the early 1980s, I was a young club professional at the Isleworth Country Club, Palmer's newest Orlando-based facility. One day Arnold decided to put me through one of his "real tests" of being a good PGA golf professional, something he required all his pros to pass at his clubs.

"Brad," he began, "I want you to take this new driver of mine and change the rubber grip to a nice leather one. And I like it stretched real *tight*."

I was a bit perplexed. *Leather? Do they really still make the stuff for grips?* I wondered. Years earlier I had taken a course on how to set an underlisting and wrap leather, but I could count on one hand how many times since I turned professional three years earlier that a member wanted me to put on leather grips. Regardless, the request had come from the King himself, and so I set out to do it.

I dutifully took the driver into the club's downstairs repair workshop to begin the job. Soon after, Isleworth's head pro, Dave O'Connor, made his way down to see how his young apprentice was doing with Arnold Palmer's new driver. Frankly, I was still having a heck of a time getting the wrap on top of the underlisting positioned correctly. Dave was kind enough to lend some help. Just then, Arnold walked through the door with a look of concern. "What seems to be taking so long?" he said with a smirk. "Here, let me show you guys how to wrap that correctly."

We could tell he was looking forward to giving us a real lesson in wrapping leather the Palmer way. Unwrapping what we had started, he said, "You have got to get this started much tighter by pulling real hard—like this!" Suddenly, *snap!* The leather ripped in half. Arnold chuckled. "I guess that was a bit too hard." With that, Arnold grabbed another strap of leather and finished the job in no time.

As soon as he was out of earshot, Dave turned to me, shaking his head in near disbelief. "Are you kidding me? Did you see that? He just ripped a leather grip in half with his bare hands!" By now the entire golf staff had gathered in the club fitting room, taking turns pulling on the other end of the ripped strap of leather, attempting this "sword in the stone"–type conquest—but to no avail.

THE IMPORTANCE OF A FIRM GRIP

Mr. Palmer's lesson of how to best shake someone's hand, by looking directly into their eyes and taking the firmest of grips, seems to be a deceptively simple gesture. Yet from where I sit, it's an important step to becoming aware of a person's character. Often we can make a connection, becoming emotionally engaged, during an introduction. Our tendency is to judge someone at face value instead of investing further time and effort getting to know with certainty who they really are.

My great friend and PGA golfer Dicky Pride recalls that Palmer's handshake nearly broke him in half even though he's bigger and taller than the legend. But the Alabama native sees the significance of the psychology behind the mere physical aspects of the handshake.

"Arnold desires to trust his instincts," Dicky wrote. "Yes, his decisions are made with due diligence. But when making the final decision, he confirms his commitment with a firm grip. How trusting is your own handshake? And perhaps just as importantly, how firm are the handshakes of those with whom you surround yourself?"[6]

There is no record of what type of handshake King Solomon handed out in biblical times. But if a firm handshake is reflective of strong character, I suspect he would have given Arnold Palmer a run for his money. "He becometh poor that dealeth with a slack hand," he once wrote, "but the hand of the diligent maketh rich."[7]

So let's heed the advice of the two kings: *give a firm handshake!*

Leave the World Better
Than You Found It

DURING MY ORIENTATION SESSION with the Arnold Palmer Golf Management Company, CEO Ed Bignon told the new hires that if we were ever around Arnold Palmer and happened to see a piece of trash lying on the ground, we'd better pick it up—or Arnie would do it for us. He might even throw a pink slip our way for good measure.

Anyone even remotely associated with Arnold Palmer will quickly learn that he's a stickler for neatness and cleanliness, especially on or around the golf course. A few years after that initial meeting with Ed, I was privileged to be paired with Arnie in the daily Shootout at Bay Hill.[1] We were enjoying the day and playing some good golf on the front nine despite rather blustery conditions. We teed off on the ninth hole and began walking down the fairway when a Snickers bar wrapper from an adjacent fairway went flying right by me at a pretty good clip. Since I was rather engrossed in the game, I didn't think anything of it and kept striding down the fairway. That turned out to be a mistake.

Suddenly I saw Arnold sprinting toward that piece of runaway trash as if it were a hundred-dollar bill. Stepping down with his size ten Johnston & Murphy golf shoes, he gaffed the wrapper with his cleats. He picked it up and turned toward me with a grin, as if he had just taken the grand prize. Fortunately, he didn't fire or even chastise me, but I'm quite sure he was confident his point was made.

> *Our obligation in life is to leave the world a better place than we found it.*
>
> CLAUDE W. AHRENS

EACH DOING OUR PART

More than a decade has passed since that windswept day, but I was recently reminded of it by a similar experience. Harris Rosen, a friend and self-made billionaire hotelier, and I were out walking one day, talking about marketing ideas for my newly opened golf school.[2] Harris stopped in mid-stride and, while continuing our conversation, bent down and picked up a napkin off the sidewalk inside Shingle Creek Golf Club in Orlando. He gently placed it in my hand; the master was again teaching the student. No words were exchanged. I just grinned as I received the point of his gesture, especially given the fond memory of that earlier lesson from Arnold Palmer.

If you're over the age of thirty, you'll probably remember a popular public service announcement featuring a "crying Indian" that ran on television stations all over the country. The ad begins with a Native American paddling his canoe up a visibly polluted river. After pulling the boat up on shore, he walks through a forested area strewn with trash. He finally winds up alongside a road where a thoughtless motorist tosses out a bag of garbage, which lands at the Native American's feet, smashing wide open. The ad concludes with a close-up shot of his face and a single tear running down his cheek. "People start pollution," an announcer says somberly. "People can stop it."[3]

As I understand it, the ad came under some criticism for exaggerating the issues, but the point was clear: Each of us has a chip in the game, and if we're willing to commit to the task of leaving things better than we originally found them, everybody benefits. If we don't, everyone suffers.

THE KING OF CHARITY

Arnold's widespread philanthropic outreach to dozens of charities ranks near the top when it comes to improving the world, and to describe Mr. Palmer as generous would be an understatement. There are the Arnold Palmer Hospitals for Children in Orlando and Latrobe, the Winnie Palmer Hospital for Women and Babies in Orlando, and the Arnold Palmer Prostate Center in Rancho Mirage, California, to name just a few.[4]

For years now, Mr. Palmer has been teaming up with Jack Nicklaus and Gary Player to raise money for a variety of charitable causes. They've become quite the trio and have garnered a reputation as the links version of the Rat Pack. In fact, in the late spring of 2010, the three men raised over $15.1 million in the single biggest fundraising day in PGA Tour history. The money was destined for the Mountain Mission School in Grundy, Virginia. The eighty-nine-year-old institution teaches three hundred children, ranging in age from eighteen months to twenty years.

It would be easy and convenient for these men to retreat to the privacy of their own homes, citing busy schedules, age, infirmity, even fatigue. By almost every measure, they've already given back more than most, but they still feel a call to give back a little more. And you know what? They have fun doing it. At the Mountain Mission School fundraiser, the three legends were miked so viewers could listen in on the friendly banter. At one point, Mr. Palmer, always the jokester, said that Gary Player, known for being frugal, was a man with deep pockets and short arms.

"Gary Player is so cheap," Mr. Palmer quipped, "he wouldn't give ducks a free drink if he owned Lake Okeechobee."

In response, Nicklaus cracked that he's heard the same stories so often that he survives by turning off his hearing aids.

Mr. Palmer has helped remind me that charitable work is not only a noble endeavor and well worth the time but it's also a way to have fun while giving back to your community.

True leaders always leave things better than they found them.

Time and example have shown me that successful people such as Arnold Palmer, Gary Player, Jack Nicklaus, and Harris Rosen do what they do in a very disciplined and precise manner each and every day. And while each of them serves in a different capacity, what they all do follows this "deceptively simple" lesson: true leaders always leave things better than they found them.

Always Play for the Love of the Game

THE COMEDIAN BOB HOPE made his living telling jokes on radio and television, and he wound up becoming a favorite of millions of American military personnel as he traveled the world entertaining the troops as part of the USO tour circuit. Bob loved to leave them laughing, but he also loved the game of golf and took every opportunity to poke fun at the foibles of his own play.

In 1985, Bob penned a book with a telling and comical title: *Bob Hope's Confessions of a Hooker: My Lifelong Affair with Golf.*[1] It's a humorous compendium of stories and quips, mostly centered on the vexing nature of his own game. Several of the entries even featured our mutual dear friend, Arnold Palmer:

> Arnie's really had a fabulous career in golf. He's won as much money as I've spent on lessons.
>
> He [Arnold Palmer] told me how I could cut eight strokes off my score ... skip one of the par 3s.
>
> Palmer used to be a professional golfer, but now he's a conglomerate. He has so many irons in the fire he has to play the tour with his woods.
>
> I sometimes wonder if Palmer isn't getting too involved with TV commercials. When he missed a putt the other day, he put the ball back and said, "Take two."[2]

But knowing that many a truth is often spoken in jest, I've always found this next quote from Bob Hope to be strikingly candid, clear, and representative of how the average player feels about the sport: "Golf is a funny game," Hope once reflected. "It's done much for health, and at the same time has ruined people by robbing them of their peace of mind. Look at me; I'm the healthiest idiot in the world!"[3]

> *Play is where life lives, where the game is the game. At its borders, we slip into heresy, become serious, lose our sense of humor, fail to see the incongruities of everything we hold to be important . . . and we lose the good life and the good things that play provides.*[4]
>
> CARDIOLOGIST AND WRITER
> GEORGE SHEEHAN

IN PURSUIT OF PERSPECTIVE

Talking and working with professional golfers behind the scenes, away from the glare of the klieg lights and the eager pens of journalists, I can testify to just how difficult it is for professionals to manage and navigate the swings of professional fortune.

Many of my clients nearly live or die with each shot and often drag their feelings — both negative and positive — into how they perceive themselves outside of golf. When they win, all is wonderful and right with the world. But even for a star, winning tournaments is a relatively rare occurrence. I've noticed that negative vibrations tend to resonate much longer than do the thrills of victory. Somebody once told me they think this roller-coaster nature of the game is why the Scots invented the nineteenth hole "to take ye sting out of ye bite."

The story of Russian novelist Fyodor Dostoevsky's brush with death remains one of the greatest examples of just how powerful a jolt of perspective can be. In 1849 Dostoevsky was sentenced to death by a Russian court for a series of supposed anti-government activities. Soon after, on December 22, he was led into a large courtyard, hooded, and told he was to be killed by firing squad.[5] As he stood there waiting to die, his mind raced back through the years. *So this was how life was to end?* But suddenly, from the distance, he heard the sound of a bugler signaling retreat. Inexplicably, Dostoevsky's life had been spared! His death sentence was commuted to time in a Siberian work camp, and after four years of hard labor, he was released. He then went on to achieve the literary successes for which he is known, writing and publishing *Crime and Punishment*,[6] *The Possessed*,[7] and *The Brothers Karamazov*.[8]

Chuck Colson, an author, former special counselor to President Richard Nixon, and founder of Prison Fellowship, pointed out that Fyodor Dostoevsky was given the greatest of all gifts — he was given the chance to see his end, which turned out to be the beginning of the rest of his life.[9]

On a much less dramatic level, Arnold Palmer has a penchant for sharing words of wisdom that help keep things in perspective. Although he's made his living by playing golf, he regularly urges others when they play golf to remember that it's still just a game and nothing more. Which brings me to one of my favorite conversations with Arnie.

We were together in his Latrobe office when I asked, "Mr. Palmer, you have often talked to me about the importance of keeping things in perspective and how easy it can be to lose perspective in playing this game. How did *you* keep it simple?"

"Well," he replied, "my father always taught me that golf is a game, and we should always play it like a game and enjoy it. I've always played golf as hard as I could, just like you play football or anything else you've done. And when you forget that it's a game, you end up in more trouble than you are looking for. It's a game, play it like a game, go for what you can go for, and make it something that you really enjoy doing."

He said, " 'Going for it' intrigued me. It raised my interests to do the things that I did when playing golf. I tried to be bold and have fun taking on the challenge of a risk-reward shot that I felt I could pull off in my mind. 'Going for it' inspired me further to pull off the challenging shots, especially when I needed them the most—for the win!"

Understanding how to approach our challenges "carpe diem" can often bring back the excitement and energy required to climb our mountains with childlike playfulness, whatever task might be required of us. Back in 1978, George Sheehan penned *Running and Being*,[10] a runaway bestseller that helped spark the first great running boom. Three years earlier, Sheehan was beginning to work through this concept of taking a game seriously— but still keeping its pursuit in perspective. He wrote:

> In play you realize simultaneously the supreme importance and the utter insignificance of what you are doing. You accept the paradox of pursuing what is at once essential and inconsequential. In play you can totally commit yourself to a goal that minutes later is completely forgotten.
>
> Play, then, is the answer to the puzzle of our existence, the stage for our excesses and exuberances. Violence and dissent are part of its joy. Territory is defended with every ounce of our strength and determination, and moments later we are embracing our opponents and delighting in the game that took place.[11]

Young Arnie was very fortunate to have a father who poured this type of wisdom and perspective into his mind at such an early age. Deacon Palmer's counsel was good for Arnie, and it's good for us too: Find enjoyment in your play, revel in what you're able to do, and stop worrying about what you can't do. And if you ever lose the love of the game, the problem is probably not the game; the problem is more likely your *definition* of the game itself.

If you ever lose the love of the game, the problem is probably not the game; the problem is more likely your definition of the game.

Get the Ball to the Hole

WHEN IT COMES TO living life to its fullest, consider trying to employ one of the great philosophies of putting: never up, never in. In other words, unless you hit the ball hard enough on the green, it'll never have a chance of making it to the cup.

So it goes with life: Dare to be aggressive enough and you'll not only give yourself a chance to reach your goal, but you'll also begin finding your way toward reaching your fullest potential. Conversely, approaching things with apathy and constant reservation will always leave you wanting and rarely, if ever, satisfied. Whoever said there's nothing harder than the softness of indifference was right. There's a good reason why Nike has made billions from its "Just do it!" advertising campaign. The philosophy is incredibly effective.

> *Putting is like wisdom — partly a natural gift and partly the accumulation of wisdom.*[1]
>
> ARNOLD PALMER

A ROUND WITH THE KING

Fresh off of the Flagler College golf team and onto the Florida mini-tours, I was playing the best golf of my young adult life, and, at the Bay Hill Shootout in December 1985, I was paired for my first round with the legend and King, Arnold Palmer.

Frankly, I was so nervous to be playing in the same group as Mr. Palmer, I couldn't even feel my hands.

Although it's been twenty-six years, I still remember every detail about stepping up to that first hole. It was a par five that was around 500 yards (and since has been turned into a 461-yard par four). The tee box was just a few steps off the porch of the pro shop, and at the appointed time, Arnold came bounding down the stairs. Royce Nielson, Arnie's faithful and longtime caddie, handed him his driver. The King wasted little time and went straight to work. His first swing of the day resulted in a perfect draw around the corner, the ball landing squarely in the middle of the fairway.

Now it was my turn. Silently struggling with a sensation nearing hyperventilation, I was somehow able to get the ball balanced on the tee peg despite my shaking fingers. *Just do what you saw his ball do*, I remember thinking to myself, *and swing smooth*. I took my swing, looked up, and, to my great relief, saw the ball tracking on a perfect line. Believe it or not, it came to rest in the middle of the fairway—some twenty yards past Palmer's first shot! He turned around to give me a look. The "Arnold Palmer look" is something that I've grown accustomed to over the years. It's something of a mix between a steely-eyed glare and a look of pure disgust. One thing is certain: my boss knew how to shake you up without ever saying a word. In this instance, was he joking? It was hard to tell. Arnie has a good poker face. Looking back now, I'm sure he was having some fun with me. I can recall thinking how fortunate that my twenty-four-year-old body, jacked with adrenaline, happened to align with all the forces of the universe for that one perfect moment in time! Royce hurried past to catch up with Palmer's giant stride, turned toward me, and said with a smile and a wink, "*Breathe*, man!"

My approach shot fell short of the green by five yards and

rolled into the front bunker with the pin cut just over the lip. I was about to play out when I took one more look at the flag to see a polished pair of Johnston & Murphy shoes standing on the top of the bunker's edge. Arnold was hovering so close that I could almost feel the vibration of his presence. I was now tense again, thinking, *Nothing cute here, Brad; just get it out and don't mess up!* I swung, and by the grace of God, the sand-blasted ball came to rest within two feet of the hole. When it came my time to putt, Arnold said those ever-encouraging words golfing buddies like to add prior to that most important stroke: "Don't miss it." Fortunately, I didn't and, miraculously, birdied the hole.

After we teed off on number two, Mr. Palmer seemed to become preoccupied with the businessmen who had joined us that day. He loves to talk shop and always seemed to be on the hunt for a new business opportunity. I was grateful for the distraction, kept to myself, and kept playing, trying to focus on avoiding an embarrassing mistake.

On the number seven tee box, Mr. Palmer turned to me and said, "Brad, do you know that you are five under par?"

I really had no idea. Caught up in the moment and not wanting to look bad in front of this man I admired so much, I was playing out of my head. The next time we exchanged words was walking down the eighteenth fairway. "You know, son," he said to me, followed by an extended pause, "you have a nice game. But you really must stay aggressive when you're playing well and learn to always just get the ball to the hole."

What? I thought. *I'm five under par! That's a darn good score!* But as I reviewed my round, I concluded that he was right—especially over the final four holes. My unconscious mindset was to finish without losing ground. As a result, I wound up leaving several birdie attempts short instead of charging to keep on "going for broke."

You miss 100 percent of the shots you never take.

WAYNE GRETZKY

Whether on the golf course, at your place of employment, or in your personal pursuit of your faith, you must, in the words of Palmer, boldly play to win. "Go big or go home!" some like to say. They're right. Be aggressive. Be bold. Take calculated risks.

MAKING IT PERSONAL

Polls and studies routinely show that most people are conservative by nature. We loathe change and run toward the predictable even if it's not comfortable. In doing so, I wonder how often we're missing out on a great adventure.

I once heard a story about a man who stopped in a country store in a small town in Georgia, one of those great old buildings with high ceilings and wooden floors. In the middle of the floor was an aging Labrador retriever that kept moaning and groaning, but neither the owner nor the customers paid any attention to him.

Finally, the traveler asked the shopkeeper, "Is there something wrong with your dog?"

"Nah," he replied, "that's Buster. He's just sitting on a nail."

"Why doesn't he move?" the man inquired.

"I guess it hurts him enough to moan but not enough to move."

I sometimes think the same could be said of us. We gripe and groan, but rarely do we do anything to change the source of our complaint. We're not thrilled with our lot, but for some reason, we're satisfied with the status quo. Just as in the game of golf, there's a tendency in life to play it safe, fearing we might overshoot the green or lose our best new ball in the lake.

Don't believe that lie.

Edwin Friedman, a sociologist and author of the book *A Failure of Nerve: Leadership in the Age of the Quick Fix*, looked at the problems plaguing modern society—from the classroom to the boardroom to the dinner table at home. Friedman's main premise was stunningly simple: too many Americans have lost their nerve because they've lost their love of imagination and the unconventional.

To illustrate his thesis, Friedman pointed to the world that framed Christopher Columbus's 1492 expedition—a Europe struggling with a general malaise caused by a combination of political, social, economic, and theological downers. Yet from that cultural malaise, Columbus emerged and, with a single act of bravery, discovered the New World. Europe was suddenly "all agog," its long-standing depression lifted "like a morning mist," Friedman wrote. "Novelty began to shine everywhere," and the seeds of the Renaissance took root.[2]

All because Christopher Columbus took a chance.

All because Christopher Columbus made the effort to try.

All because Christopher Columbus rejected the old way of doing things and dared to believe what others did not. And he did something.

Are you stuck in a rut? Are you caught up in a frustrating cycle? It takes guts to get out of ruts. Imagination is often more important than knowledge. Maybe it's time to let yourself think new thoughts and dream new dreams.

You Get Out of It
What You Put Into It

BACK WHEN I WAS the director of the Arnold Palmer Golf Academy based out of the Bay Hill Club in Orlando, my days began at 7:00 a.m., Monday through Saturday. The school opened promptly at 8:00 a.m., and I can still remember how one new freshman mini-tour player would be the first young professional on the practice range by early morning light and always one of the last to leave at dusk. That player was someone who would become my good friend and a PGA Tour winner, Dicky Pride.

Dicky's work ethic was well beyond that of any of the other mini-tour players preparing to go to Tour School in the fall. I also noticed he possessed a strong self-confidence and a willingness to talk openly and candidly about his abilities. Some of the other players didn't like his attitude. They considered him to be cocky, not confident. Frankly, I was always a bit amused at his strong ego. I thought it showed a great degree of determination, and though his game may not have yet caught up to his mouth, he was declaring exactly what he wanted to accomplish. I admired that about him. He certainly had learned the positive mindset of the PGA champions who were playing out of Bay Hill at that time. Swinging alongside him were greats such as Payne Stewart, Scott Hoch, Greg Norman, Corey Pavin, Mark O'Meara, Ian Baker-Finch, and Brad Faxon, to name just a few.

With every deed you are sowing a seed, though the harvest you may not see.

ELLA WHEELER WILCOX

In my honest opinion, Dicky wasn't the best player to ever show up at Bay Hill with the aspirations of playing on the PGA Tour. In fact, in the summer of 1992, Bay Hill was swimming with young aspiring talent preparing for Tour School in the fall. At that time, Dicky was realistically about the eighth or ninth best player in that group of professionals and amateurs.

Since college, one of Dicky's coaches has been the world-renowned sports psychologist Bob Rotella. Preparing Dicky for Qualifying School, Rotella had given him a bit of advice similar to that which I had given to Bradley Hughes. It worked for Dickey just as it had for Bradley. (Dicky told me it gave him a boost of confidence and led to quick success on the Tour.) Rotella told him, "Q-school is going to be a little easier than playing the Tommy Armour Tour has been for you because not so many players really believe they can do well at the Tour Qualifying."

Well, that just fired up Dicky's already confident attitude and gave him an extra kick at just the right time. Pride and seven other Bay Hill junior members headed to the grinding test known as the PGA Tour Qualifying School that fall of 1992. Only two made it through with full exempt cards: Robert Damron and Dicky Pride. Everyone at the club was anticipating Robert's success. He had proven himself in the National Amateur events and mini-tours since turning professional. But nobody was expecting such a stellar performance from Mr. Pride—except Dicky.

I've asked the forty-one-year-old Tuscaloosa native to share a story about his first meeting with our mutual friend, Arnold Palmer. According to Dicky, the meeting he writes about turned out to be one of those life-changing conversations that came at just the right time. To this day he remains amazed how a casual and offhand conversation came to inspire him to remarkable success on the PGA Tour.

A TURNING POINT
Dicky Pride

As I watched Arnold Palmer come off the steps of the pro shop, my mind and heart began to race. How would I address him? What would I say? I knew I was overthinking things, but how do you properly and respectfully address a legend?

I decided to be straightforward and direct. Greeting him on the putting green, I walked up, stuck out my hand, and said simply, "Mr. Palmer, Dicky Pride. I just wanted to thank you very much for allowing me to become a junior member. I really appreciate the opportunity."

Mr. Palmer, ever the gentleman, even though he had likely heard a variation of that comment hundreds of times, was polite and gracious. "Oh, good, good," he replied with a smile. "Now, Dicky, you're going to try to turn pro, aren't you?"

"Yes, sir," I replied. "I'm about to turn pro, and try to play . . . see what I can do."

Mr. Palmer paused, placed one hand on his hip and the other on his club. "Well, do you mind if I give you some advice?"

Here was one of my dad's idols and the "King of golf" himself, and he wanted to give me some advice? I was sweating bullets. "Oh, yes, sir, please do!" I replied eagerly.

"You know, Dicky," he began, "when you are on tour—" He stopped suddenly, clearly aware that I was hanging on every word. He cocked his head, a sign, I later learned, that he was deadly serious. "There are no miracles in this game of golf. You only get out of it what you put into it."

With that bit of advice, we immediately connected. It was the same no-nonsense wisdom that my father taught me about working hard and giving my full energy toward what I wanted to achieve.

Parting ways, I can remember spinning on my heels and releasing the air that was trapped in my lungs. I immediately ran into the pro shop. Throwing myself onto the counter, I hollered to nobody in particular, "I need a sheet of paper and pen!" The three assistant pros behind the counter gave me puzzled looks.

"Excuse me?" one asked quizzically.

I repeated myself a bit more slowly. "I need a sheet of paper and a pen. I've got to write something down!"

I still have that "Palmerism" scribbled on that paper in my office for daily viewing:

"There are no miracles in this game of golf. You only get out of it what you put into it."

For the last eighteen years, those simple words have helped to frame my pursuit of professional golf. I've begun every day with one goal: try to improve my game from yesterday. I may not always make it, but I'm going to give it a shot.

Dicky's story is a great testimonial to the benefits of working toward your goal on a daily basis, for within two years of that first conversation with Arnie, Dicky went on to win the Federal Express St. Jude Classic.[1] He's since had more than a dozen top-ten finishes in PGA Tour events with over $3 million in career earnings.[2]

There are no miracles in this game of golf. You only get out of it what you put into it.

ARNOLD PALMER

In order to get something out of life, we must put something in. It's true, isn't it? When children complain about not getting anything out of school, chances are they are not putting anything into it. When we complain about a boring coworker or an unfriendly neighbor, we so often forget that it's a two-way street. You have to bring something to the table if you hope to fully enjoy the feast. Our efforts and actions matter; there is a consequence (and a benefit) to putting every ounce of energy toward the task.

An old Chinese proverb says, "If a man plants melons, he will reap melons; if he sows beans, he will reap beans."[3]

Back around AD 50 or 60, when the apostle Paul wrote to the Galatians, a group living in what is now the central part of Turkey, just south of the Black Sea, he emphasized the principles of a proactive approach to life:

A man reaps what he sows. The one who sows to please his sinful nature, from that nature will reap destruction; the one who sows to please the Spirit, from the Spirit will reap eternal life. Let us not become weary in doing good, for at the proper time we will reap a harvest if we do not give up.

GALATIANS 6:7–9

Paul, Arnold, and Dicky—three very different men with different talents and goals—have each come to the same conclusion: you get out of it what you put into it.

PART 2

YOUR STARTING POINT INFLUENCES YOUR DESTINATION

Success in golf and life depends less on strength of body
than upon strength of mind and character.

ARNOLD PALMER

WHEN I WAS A young man, my father was our hometown's county attorney, and he had two sayings to make a point regarding my choice of certain friends. The first was: "If you lie down with dogs, you will get fleas." The second was obviously culled from his professional experience: "Regarding the law, there is guilt by association."

He was correct, of course. Without directly coming out and saying so, my father was strongly suggesting that my choice of friends was bound to influence the direction of my life. (Thanks, Dad!)

Before we head into the next lesson, I'd like you to take a moment to run an inventory of who is in your life. Are the people in your life operating on the same frequency? Do you share similar goals? Are they influencing you in a positive or a negative way? Do they feed your mind with inspiration, perspiration, or desperation? Are they supportive of your dreams and goals? Do they "walk the walk" and lead by example — or are they just big talkers? After spending time together, are you energized or exhausted?

My study of and coaching experience with high-performance

athletes have given me a clear indication of how the best are inspired by the best. Greatness is not caught—but greatness does draw talent together. Back in 1963, President John F. Kennedy touched on this subject when he pointed out that "a rising tide lifts all the boats." He was speaking of diplomatic relationships between nations, but he could just as well have been speaking about the benefits of surrounding yourself with friends who think positively. "A partnership, by definition," he said at the time, "serves both partners, without domination or unfair advantage."[1]

Those athletes whom I classify as "high performers" are also quite willing to encourage others to believe in their dream. They all seem to enjoy helping and encouraging others to take action toward self-improvement.

The following stories and interviews explore how Arnold Palmer was inspired by other great performers.

Tap Into the Power of Imagination

ON ANY GIVEN SUNDAY afternoon of childhood, my younger brother and I could pick up two sticks off the lawn and begin the greatest pirate sword duel in the history of the world. He was the scar-faced Captain Hook, and I was usually a swash-buckling hero from any number of Errol Flynn movies.

All too often—or so it seemed—I carried this same penchant for fantasy thoughts to school with me. I can recall being "interrupted" by my second-grade teacher, Miss McCowan. She would slap my desk with her ruler, snapping me back into reality and scaring me half to death in the process. In some ways, I was like Ralphie Parker, the blond-haired boy from the seasonal cult-favorite movie *A Christmas Story*.[1]

Everybody remembers Ralph. There he sat in Miss Shield's second-grade classroom, resting his elbow on the desk and his chin in the palm of his hand as he stared off into space. We see him dreaming of being a cowboy and saving his family from certain torture and death—all thanks to the sharpshooting precision of his "Red Ryder, carbine-action, two-hundred-shot range model air rifle."[2] In many ways, that was me! At times I would dream about rescuing the world from disaster. During other moments, mostly as I grew older and began to zero in on my dream, I would imagine myself walking the lush fairways of Augusta National. The green jacket was a perfect fit.

But sadly, for too many of us, there comes a point in life when we cease to dream and begin to think only in logical, straight lines. We might hear folks say things such as, "It's about time for you to quit daydreaming. Grow up and deal with reality. Start acting more mature and responsible." Regrettably, many grudgingly agree.

I'm reminded of the wonderfully inspirational film *Rudy*.[3] Based on a true story, it featured the pursuit of five-foot, six-inch, 165-pound Daniel "Rudy" Ruettiger's dream of playing football for the University of Notre Dame.[4] The film's tagline says it all: "Sometimes a winner is a dreamer who just won't quit."[5] Amen!

Sometimes a winner is a dreamer who just won't quit.
TAGLINE FROM THE MOVIE *RUDY*

One of the more memorable scenes takes place in a high school classroom when a teacher catches the Joliet, Illinois, native daydreaming—likely about football—when he should have been paying attention to the lesson. "The problem with dreamers," the teacher says to a now-downtrodden Ruettiger, "is that they usually aren't doers."[6] Fortunately for Rudy and the rest of us rooting along, the teacher was ultimately proved wrong.

COUNTERING THE JOY KILLERS

The teacher in *Rudy* is representative of all those people whose paths we cross who can't help but sow discouragement. This is partly because certain segments of society teach us that unless you want to be an actor or artist, you have to stop "pretending" and focus on "real" professions or legitimate, marketable interests.

I've always suspected that Arnold Palmer was a dreamer. After all, to look at his career, including his vast fortune and the incredible scope of the corporate outreach, I can't help but think he embodies the perspective of George Bernard Shaw. Senator

Bobby Kennedy is often credited with this line, but it was Shaw who first wrote, "Some men see things that are and ask why. I dream things that never were and ask why not."[7] As someone who sees Palmer up close, I'm quite confident in saying the man is the embodiment of this ideal. Keying off this subject, I decided to ask Arnie whether he daydreamed as a kid.

"Yes, I suppose you could say that," he responded wistfully. "During my childhood, I would daydream, like kids do, about playing against the greatest golfers of that era: Ben Hogan, Sam Snead, Walter Hagan, and certainly Bobby Jones. Jones left a positive impression with me, and I often thought about meeting him and certainly competing against him. I never had a chance to compete against him because he had already retired, but I certainly enjoyed many good experiences with Bobby Jones for several years as I began to play in the Masters after my U.S. Amateur victory until his death in December of 1971. When we did finally meet, I'm sure that my childhood daydreaming gave me a similar experience that you are saying happened to you as well. This could also be one of the reasons why the Masters Tournament always felt so good to me and was the tournament above all others that I really desired to win."

In many ways, Arnie was employing the tried and true practice of "positive mental imaging,"[8] which is really just a fancy way of saying that he envisioned what he wanted to accomplish—and over time methodically and deliberately worked to make it come true.

Jack Nicklaus, Palmer's longtime friend and rival, regularly practiced positive mental imaging. Here is how he described his technique:

I never hit a shot even in practice without having a sharp in-focus picture of it in my head. It's like a color movie.

First, I "see" the ball where I want it to finish, nice and white and sitting up high on the bright green grass. Then the scene quickly changes, and I "see" the ball going there: its path, trajectory, and shape, even its behavior on landing. Then there's a sort of fade-out, and the next scene shows me making the kind of swing that will turn the previous images into reality. Only at the end of this short private Hollywood spectacular do I select a club and step up to the ball.[9]

With eighteen major championships and 115 professional wins,[10] Nicklaus, the "Golden Bear," clearly settled on a method that worked wonders for him.

What Age Do You Imagine *Yourself*?

Prior to his death in 2007, Ed Seay was Mr. Palmer's business partner and chief architect in Arnold Palmer Design Company.[11] Over the last thirty-five years, the company has built over two hundred golf courses around the globe. Arnold and Ed traveled together, worked together, and played together for the majority of their adult lives. Shortly after I began working for the Palmer organization, I was at dinner with Ed. Assuming the best way to learn about someone is talking with the people who know that person best, I began asking him about Mr. Palmer.

"You know, Brad," Ed said, "Arnold is just a big kid at heart. Even at the age of fifty-five, he thinks he is twenty-five."

Ed was right. Anyone who closely observes Mr. Palmer will affirm there's a youthfulness that permeates his spirit. Now at just over eighty years young, Arnold is the first to admit that the physical prowess of twenty-five is a thing of the past. Nevertheless, with a twinkle in his eye and a smirk on his face, he'll gladly accept a challenge from any of his Bay Hill Shootout buddies. The young guys quickly learn that Arnold Palmer imagines he's still that kid at Latrobe Country Club who had big dreams and high hopes of one day competing against his hero, Bobby Jones, in the U.S. Open.

THE IMPORTANCE OF DREAMS

If you think your imagination needs to be turned back on, I highly recommend you consider unlocking your inner child so you can dream new dreams. Yes, that's right. It's time to develop and strengthen your God-given mental faculties by starting with perhaps the most important one: your imagination.

For most of us, it's been lying dormant for years. But like a young Arnie, with a gun strapped to his side, taking aim during Ladies Day at Latrobe, dare to dream again. Exercise your imagination to open yourself again to all you're capable of. Return to the joy and hope that are part of having faith in the journey ahead. Then take steps toward accomplishing the dream laid on your heart.

Developing the Master's Touch

THROUGHOUT HIS LONG AND STORIED career, Arnold Palmer has always been quick to give credit where credit was due—especially when attributing reasons for his own fame and success. Whether he had just won another major tournament, finished high on the money list, or closed a multi-million-dollar business deal, Palmer has suggested his achievements have only been due to the fact that he is standing on the shoulders of giants.[1]

In some ways, he reminds me of the little boy who was riding atop his father's shoulders. The pair met up with an uncle who hadn't visited in nearly a year.

"Oh my," the man said to the tyke in jest, "how you've grown!"

Being the literalist that little children can be, the boy said with great seriousness, "Well, you know, Uncle Joe, not all of this is me."

Topping Arnie's list of giants would have to be his parents, Deacon and Doris Palmer. I've heard him tell dozens of stories about both of them during my tenure, but the anecdotes are especially rich when it comes to his father. "Arnold's feelings toward him [Deacon]," wrote biographer Ian O'Connor, "were always found at the intersection of respect and admiration, love and fear."[2] Deacon hailed from a generation when fathers tended to be a bit more emotionally stoic. Arnie always knew his dad loved him, but he might not have heard it as much as he did from his mother. Arnold's sister, Sandy, once said their mom was "the soft part of the team."[3] Doris adored Arnie and loved to brag about her celebrity son.

For a long time I was curious about who else might be on Palmer's list of mentors. One afternoon, sitting in his sun-splashed Latrobe office, I finally asked.

ARNOLD'S INSPIRATION

"I know Deacon Palmer was certainly your mentor," I said. "He taught you how to play the game, and he taught you how to treat people with respect. Mark McCormack [Palmer's promoter] came into your life at just the right moment and did amazing things for you in the business world. President Eisenhower was also a dear friend. It goes without saying that your late wife of forty-five years, Winnie, was your other (better) half. These are key people that I know were involved in your successful journey in golf, business, and life—though I know you can't separate those areas from each other."

Arnie sat patiently. I was taking a little too long to arrive at my question, but I was eager to lay its foundation.

Leaning forward, I said, "My question is this: Beyond these key and beloved individuals, was there anyone else who really inspired you to not only dream—but to dream and think *big*?"

"Well," he began, "all of those people you mentioned certainly had influence. Winnie was a major support system for me. She knew my moods, and she would help with my attitude and outlook. My conversations with Ike, President Eisenhower, were good and helpful. I enjoyed his company. His attitude and positive outlook were always an inspiration to me.

I cannot teach anybody anything. I can only make them think.
SOCRATES

"I read Bobby Jones's book [*The Rights and Wrongs of Golf*[4]] when I was a young boy growing up, and I got some positive things out of that on how to win. Another book that I read was Byron Nelson's *Winning Golf,*[5] and it had a very positive ring to it too. He put so much thought into his golf swing, calculating what he wanted to do in hitting a golf ball. He put blueprints in the book of his golf swing and what he was doing, though I didn't swing anything like Byron Nelson. If you remember, Nelson dipped a little when he hit the golf ball, and I never dipped in my life. I created a style of my own. I took how he created his swing and transferred it to my way, building my own golf swing around the fundamentals that my father, Deacon, taught me as a boy."

IN SEARCH OF THE BEST

I've always been intrigued by Mr. Palmer's habit of pulling from a wide array of resources and finding what he thought was the very "best of the best" out there, blending those elements into his own way of doing things. Where some might idolize and emulate to the point of blind imitation, Arnold Palmer has always been keen to make a path his own.

Do you quickly dismiss or discount someone's ability to teach you something for superficial or non-substantive reasons? I once heard of someone who refused to listen to a pastor preach a sermon simply because the pastor was from New York City. This person apparently loathed city dwellers, believing they were snobby and arrogant, so he resisted an invitation to attend a particular church service. I wonder what he missed that morning.

On an airplane flight, an older man was speaking with a skeptical new friend about church. This "missionary" invited the person to come to his church, but the seatmate declined. Why? He explained that he was afraid he'd have to give up the religious traditions of his youth. I loved the missionary's response: "Bring all the good you already have," he told him calmly, "and let's see if we might add to it."

When reviewing the gifts and talents of his peers, whether on the golf course or in a business boardroom, that's exactly what Arnold Palmer has done his entire career.

FOLLOW THE LEADERS

Jack Nicklaus and Arnold Palmer, archrivals and dear friends, enjoy one of the warmest relationships in professional sports. Given Palmer's age, Nicklaus has always considered Arnie to be a mentor of his—not just on the golf course, but off it too. Jack once said that Arnie told him he always wrote handwritten notes of thanks to the sponsors who helped him put on his annual tournament. "So every tournament I ever played in, I always dropped the sponsor a note," Nicklaus said.[6] After studying another master of gratitude, Nicklaus enjoyed a phenomenal response to this gentlemanly action. Somebody once said that values aren't taught—they're caught.

Arnold Palmer's style of improving himself is a critical piece of the success puzzle. We all need to maintain our own identity, knowing that we're special individuals with a unique set of gifts, but do as Arnold Palmer has done. Study the masters, finding all the good they possess—and then enjoy creating your own true masterpiece called you!

Plan to Win

AUGUSTA NATIONAL IS GOLF's Garden of Eden, a stunningly beautiful slice of the American South. "If there's a golf course in heaven," Gary Player once remarked, "I hope it's like Augusta National. I just don't want an early tee time."[1]

People who visit Augusta often remark that so much of it is so green—the grass, of course, but also the benches, the bleachers, and the scoreboards. Even the sandwiches at the concession stands are traditionally wrapped in green paper. But not everything is green. In spring, the flaming red and pink azaleas hug the fairways and frame the tee boxes, providing picture-perfect images.

Enthusiasts are drawn to this exclusive course for its rhythms and traditions. First opened in 1933, the club was built on the site of an indigo plantation. There is the old white clubhouse with its wide porches, and the large oak tree, estimated to be around 150 years old,[2] near the first tee, under whose shade fans and writers still gather. One rather interesting landmark of the course is the "Eisenhower Tree" located near the seventeenth hole. As the story goes, President Dwight Eisenhower apparently hit that particular tree so many times he petitioned the club to cut it down. Augusta's leadership diplomatically rejected the request.

IN SYNC WITH HIS PLAN TO WIN

With four wins at the Masters Tournament (1958, 1960, 1962, and 1964),[3] Arnold Palmer has become synonymous with

Augusta National. For Arnie, the place seemed to fit him like a glove — or a neatly trimmed blazer. Four green jackets, two runners-up, and fourteen top-ten finishes over a fifteen-year span made me believe Palmer was in some kind of a spiritual harmony with Augusta National. I once asked him why he believed he was so successful on that course when it seemed to bring so many other gifted players to their knees.

"Well," Arnold replied with a half-cocked smile, "of course, the Masters was the tournament I really wanted to win in my life. It was the people as much as it was the place itself that made Augusta National so special to me. People like Bobby Jones and Clifford Roberts, who I became close to over the years, were an inspiration for me, not just for the golf, but for the way they conducted their lives and what they did in business too. I won the Masters in '58, but in '59 I should have won it, and I kind of let it slip a little bit. My win in 1960 was a major deal with good drama from my charging finish. Making birdies on the last two holes to win was sort of a reaction to previous situations that I was in. I just told myself that I wasn't going to let what happened that last year happen again. It inspired me to go for it and I finished strong and won."

His memories of nearly fifty years earlier still clear, he said, "My win in 1962 was a playoff and a squeeze down to the end. Then, of course, my mindset was that I had to win the Masters again, and I wanted to win one where I could walk up eighteen with the feeling of total enjoyment for having played in the tournament and having the things happen the way that I envisioned them to happen. I always wanted to have a good lead coming down the stretch with no doubt that victory was mine."

"So did you ever accomplish that particular goal?" I asked.

"It did happen that way in '62," he said with a smile, "exactly how I had seen it happening in my mind. I stood on the seventy-second hole and said to my playing partner, Dave Marr, 'I think I can win from here.' It was not offered boastfully, but as someone who had really gotten to where they wanted to get to. Then Dave, who was a good friend, kidded me. 'Make twelve!' he said. By then I could smile, knowing that I wasn't going to make twelve and that I was going to win the Masters. That victory in the very way I had envisioned it was a new and different personal satisfaction. It was something I'd been driving for in my life."

WORK YOUR PLAN

"Plan your work and work your plan." It sounds simple enough, doesn't it? Catchy too. After studying Arnold Palmer's career, I can say with assurance that the King has taken this philosophy to heart. But can the rest of us mere amateurs really believe that people can do what they desire, plan, and picture in their mind? The idea of "positive mental imaging" might not be a fail-safe exercise, but Palmer's success and the success of countless others who employ the technique suggest to me that it holds great promise.

Winning the Masters was a strong desire for Arnie, but it happened partly because he planned out how he would win and then rehearsed his plan over and over again, like an actor memorizing a script. This same technique works outside of golf—perhaps even more effectively. It's a wise person who plots a course of action before actually taking the plunge.

One of my favorite people was John Wooden, UCLA's Hall of Fame basketball coach who died in June of 2010 at the age of ninety-nine. Coach Wooden was well-known as a planner who planned his work and worked his plan. He believed strongly in preparation because he felt it gave athletes the best chance of success. Coach Wooden, like Arnold Palmer, was also a stickler for not just doing—but doing things well. He once remarked, "If you don't have time to do it right, when will you have time to do it over?" He also was a realist. "Things turn out best," he said, "for those who make the best of the way things turn out."

Certainly for Arnold Palmer, the difference between victory and defeat often came down to the time and effort he took plotting out a pretournament plan of action. Of all the things Arnold Palmer did on a consistent basis, he did one thing prior to every round of golf—something all of us should do:

He planned to win!

Trust but Verify

PRESIDENT RONALD REAGAN HAD a favorite phrase to describe his philosophy when dealing with the now former Soviet Union: "*Doveryai, no proveryai*"—trust, but verify.[1] Soviet Prime Minister Mikhail Gorbachev once said to Reagan of his use of the phrase, "You repeat that at every meeting!" America's fortieth president responded unapologetically, "I like it."[2]

Arnold Palmer and President Reagan were friends—they once played together at a Pro-Am tournament[3]—and when it came to matters of business (or politics) and the need to forge trustworthy alliances, they saw things much the same way. Trust was key, something the King followed with disciplined action as he birthed and grew Arnold Palmer Enterprises. Money was important, but the people with whom he surrounded himself drove each and every deal. If Arnie didn't feel as though he could trust a person, he just wouldn't do business with him or her.

> *Trust men and they will be true to you; treat them greatly and they will show themselves great.*
>
> RALPH WALDO EMERSON

THE PEBBLE BEACH DREAM TEAM

In 1998, legendary film actor and producer Clint Eastwood and two successful business men, Dick Ferris and Peter Ueberroth, partnered with Arnold Palmer to purchase one of America's golfing gems, Pebble Beach Properties. The scenic masterpiece known as the Pebble Beach Golf Links is one of God's finest creations. Called "The Greatest Meeting of Land and Water in the World,"[4] it is also one of the most challenging courses I've ever played. I've often joked with my golfing friends that when we meet St. Peter in heaven, he will ask, "Did you take the time to play Pebble Beach—and what did you think of the number seven hole into the teeth of a brisk Pacific Ocean breeze?" For those who haven't had the privilege of playing the course, the seventh hole is a little postage stamp of turf only 112 yards away from the pin. In my opinion, anyone who can knock it down with a five iron deserves an eternal membership in the "Almighty Golf Club." Kidding aside, Pebble Beach is certainly one of the unique spiritual experiences (golfer or not), never to be forgotten.

Mr. Palmer's decision to invest in the Pebble Beach Company and partner with Eastwood, Ferris, and Ueberroth intrigued me. Why Pebble Beach, and why these men?

I've always been a big fan of Clint Eastwood, both as an actor and director. Ueberroth's impressive portfolio, both as chairman of the United States Olympic Committee and later as commissioner of major league baseball, speaks for itself. I'm most familiar with Arnold's third partner and good friend, Dick Ferris, former CEO of United Airlines. Over the years, I've benefited from his business counsel during my years operating Arnold Palmer Academies. Given my role as company director within Arnold Palmer Enterprises, we often refer to Ferris as one of the "Three Wise Men." Dick is a brilliant adviser, capable of simplifying a complex problem. It's no wonder that he and Arnold hit it off so well.

BEHIND THE DEAL
For the last quarter century, I've witnessed Mr. Palmer's cautious and reserved attitude toward real estate offerings. He's willing to

take risks, but they're almost always conservative and calculated. Why was he willing to "go for broke" on this $820 million deal back in 1999?[5]

Arnie had had opportunities to be involved with several real estate projects over the years with Palmer Management and Arnold Palmer Design Company. As a result, many had come to him and asked him to be a part of their projects too, but he'd declined most of these invitations. So I finally asked him why he got involved with Pebble Beach. "What does Pebble Beach mean to you, and why did you personally get yourself involved in such a major development?"

"Well," he said rather matter-of-factly, "it was purely a business opportunity with the right people that I have been in business with one way or another most of my life — Ferris, Ueberroth, and Eastwood. It was a project that we had been looking at and studying for many years, so when the time was right, we were ready. The decision wasn't difficult; it was a no-brainer as far as I was concerned. Pebble Beach has always been a special place for me going back to the days of the Bing Crosby Celebrity Pro-Am & Clam Bake. The place is full of history and tradition. We desire to preserve these traditions and continue to enhance one of the finest golf experiences in the world. You know, it was probably going for broke a little bit, but it was something that I felt would be a very good thing, and it has worked out wonderfully."

TRUSTWORTHY LESSONS

From this brief exchange about Palmer's Pebble Beach acquisition, I culled several key things — lessons that apply in and outside of golf:

1. Arnold has confidence in his partners — and without that level of trust in people around him, he would never have been willing to take such risk.

2. He did his homework; he studied the opportunity for a long time.
3. He was patient; the deal took several years to come together.
4. Thanks to his fastidious preparation, when the timing was right, he was ready to pull the trigger. He said it was a "no-brainer," which, of course, isn't completely true. Because he had previously invested the time and resources, the decision only seemed easy.

"Love all, trust few, do wrong to none," a somewhat cynical William Shakespeare wrote.

Arnold Palmer's perspective is a bit more optimistic: trust those you love; love those you trust—and verify your steps along the way.

Dare to Care

I FIRST MET AUSTRALIAN GOLFER Ian Baker-Finch at Sanctuary Cove, a new luxury resort being managed by the Arnold Palmer Golf Management Company. I was flattered to have been recruited from Isleworth Country Club to move to Australia as the head professional of this thirty-six-hole golf facility soon to open on the Gold Coast. At the time, Ian was the up-and-coming playing professional who had just signed as the resort's resident touring professional. It didn't take long before I was hearing "Good day, mate!" from my friend Finchy.

From humble beginnings growing up on a small farm in Nambour, a town in the foothills of Queensland, Australia, dreaming one day of winning the British Open Golf Championship (the oldest of the four major championships in golf and commonly referred to as "The Open"), Ian Baker-Finch is a grand example of a local boy who made good. His dreams of golfing greatness were sparked by three legends—Arnold Palmer, Jack Nicklaus, and Gary Player—all due to their exhibitions in the land Down Under. By watching, reading, and playing, Finch was inspired to grab hold of his goal, work hard, and never give in. He eventually went on to become the 1991 British Open champion.[1]

Over the years, the two of us have shared hundreds of experiences, from rounds on the golf course, time at the driving range, or just walking together through day-to-day life and family issues. We've also supported each other's careers, and both of us have greatly benefited from knowing and interacting with Arnold Palmer. I've invited Finchy to share a few of his recollections of his time with the King.

THE CARING KING
Ian Baker-Finch

The Australian Masters in February of 1983 was my first one-on-one visit with Arnold. We were both playing in the tournament, and I caught him in the players' car park. I told him what a positive influence he had been on my career, and he was so kind to sign a note to me that I still have today. "Dear Ian," he wrote, "all the very best with your future in golf. Sincerely, Arnold Palmer." That really meant a lot to me for the King of golf to take his time to acknowledge and encourage me.

> *People don't care how much you know until they know how much you care.*
>
> AUTHOR JOHN C. MAXWELL

Years later, when I began playing full time on the PGA Tour in America, my wife, Jenny, and our girls, Haile and Laura, and I moved to Orlando. We bought a home in Bay Hill Village and joined the Arnold Palmer Bay Hill Club. Our nearby neighbors and good friends were Payne and Tracy Stewart and Greg and Laura Norman. Tracy, Greg, and I all grew up near one another in Queensland, so on occasions we "threw a shrimp on the barbie" for our families and friends.

In 1995, I was paired with Palmer for the first two rounds of the Open at St. Andrews — Mr. Palmer's farewell British Open. The crowds were huge! They swelled in size as we came closer to the final hole, an emotional wave of farewell for a legend. As he crossed the bridge over the Swilken Burn, built during the Roman Empire,[2] there wasn't a dry eye to be found. He was emotionally drained at the end of his round as the media asked for photos. But he was ever gracious and signed a golf ball for me that I still have displayed in my office. Even though I didn't perform at a high level that day, those few hours are among my fondest memories of golf.

But Arnie cares about more than golf. His "Champions for Children" is the annual charity fundraiser benefiting the Arnold Palmer Hospitals. I've always enjoyed volunteering and supporting Arnold's institutions, and this was one of my favorites. It's been tremendously rewarding. My parents instilled in me this concept of giving back, but I would attribute Arnold's mentorship through example—of using his celebrity to give back and help others—as a motivating factor for me. I was watching. Arnold and Winnie did so much through their charities of choice and encouraged all the younger golfers and families to do the same.

One year, the "Champions for Children" charity happened to fall on my birthday. After the tournament, we were planning to celebrate at our friend Payne Stewart's house. With his colorful outfits, jazzy caps, and signature knickers, Stewart was a fan favorite and instantly recognizable. I was looking forward to the birthday party, but plans were scrapped at the last minute when Payne decided to fly off a day early to the Tour championships in Dallas. That decision proved to be a fatal one. On that day, October 25, 1999, Payne Stewart's private Learjet, en route from Orlando to Dallas, depressurized, and Stewart, along with five other people aboard, was killed.[3]

The plane, a twin-engine, high-performance $2.5 million jet, left Orlando shortly after 9:00 a.m. The pilots stopped responding to air traffic controllers less than an hour later. Air Force jets were dispatched and reported seeing iced-over windows with no sign of life inside. The plane was on autopilot. The F-16s tracked the plane for over four hours until it ran out of fuel and crashed in a South Dakota field.

That Friday was a day we all remember but want to forget. Brad and I were making the cross-over of our first nine, and we stopped to catch up in front of the pro shop. Arnold came briskly striding out of the clubhouse and gave us the grave news about Payne and his private jet. Out of respect, Palmer immediately called everyone off the golf course. The eighteen Tour players participating were all friends of Payne's. We were all in a state of shock and disbelief. Palmer mentioned that journalists were already calling the pro shop. They wanted to speak with any of us who were willing to talk, but none of us could bear the thought of talking publicly about something so emotionally upsetting. We instead went over to Payne's house to be with his wife, Tracy, and their family. It was a horrible day!

The death of Payne Stewart came as a blow to the usually measured Palmer, who called it "one of the most terrible tragedies of modern-day golf."[4] For Palmer, like most of us, the loss was personal. Palmer had always been a big part of Payne's life. Shortly after Tracy and Payne were married, they moved to Orlando and joined the Bay Hill Club, where their home for ten years was directly off the twelfth tee box. Arnold was an adviser and father figure in Payne's life, especially after Payne's own dad passed away. Arnold would remind him, just as Deacon, Arnie's father, had said,

"Let your game do the talking." Payne always took that bit of simple wisdom to heart.

Beyond the daily doses of wisdom Arnold Palmer offered, I continued to see a common characteristic woven through his life: he cared for people in life—and for their families in death.

Palmer's successful way of attracting the best, learning from them, and emulating their best attributes was also how Ian grew in his confidence and successes in golf, business, and now as one of the finest golf analysts on network television.

THE SUBTLETIES THAT GO UNSEEN

The apostle Paul urged the Colossians that they should clothe themselves with "compassion, kindness, humility, gentleness and patience" (Colossians 3:12). When you boil this principle down to its core, that's exactly what Mr. Palmer's tendency to "forget the flair—just care" is all about. It's about forgoing your own comfort for the sake of the other guy. It's thinking about yourself less and about others more.

Take, for example, the story of Ronald Reagan and his first job. Between 1926 and 1932, the young "Dutch" Reagan worked as a lifeguard on the Rock River in Dixon, Illinois. He saved seventy-seven lives during the seven summers of his service. His pay? Fifteen dollars a week, plus all the hamburgers, onions, pickles, and root beer that he wanted from the food stand by the shore. With a spirit of self-sacrifice, the young Reagan was known to lay his life on the line to ensure the safety of those entrusted to his care. It was a theme consistent over the course of his life. He never viewed public service as a stepping-stone to prosperity, but instead as a privilege of the highest order. From saving swimmers to helping stave off the threat of nuclear annihilation, the essence of Ronald Reagan always was simple: safety through strength, strength through service.

Dale Carnegie, the public-speaking and personality development pioneer of the early 1900s, summed it up perfectly: "Do things for others and you'll find your self-consciousness evaporating like morning dew on a Missouri cornfield in July."

Isn't it interesting that we see this selfless streak running through the lives of truly great men? Be it in golf, in business, or just in life, successful people care about what happens to other people. Arnold Palmer goes a step further. He genuinely cares and he invests in their lives.

The Best Attract the Best

MICHAEL JORDAN HAS BEEN retired from the NBA since 2003, but he's still considered one of the most recognizable and admired professional athletes in world history. He continues to appear in commercials and films, and, while the famous Gatorade slogan of the 1990s, "I wanna be like Mike,"[1] may no longer be in circulation, its premise still holds true. Kids still want to play basketball with the prowess and skill of Michael Jordan, captured in the lyrics of the Gatorade jingle, "Sometimes I dream he is me."[2] For decades, kids of all ages have been drawn to this living basketball legend.

In 1992, Michael Jordan came to Orlando for the NBA All-Star Games. And what does a globe-trotting sports icon do before a big game? If he's in the Orlando area and loves the game of golf as much as MJ, he plays at the Bay Hill Club & Lodge. But Jordan didn't just come to play golf—he came to play marathon golf. We're talking fifty-four holes in one day!

On this particular day, I was honored to host him and join the foursome with a friend of Michael's and a student of mine, Robert Damron. Robert had just begun his college golf career and was already named a freshman All-American at the University of Central Florida. At the time of this writing, he was in his fifteenth season on the PGA Tour and a multi-winner.[3] Needless to say, it was a very good thing having him as my partner for the day. (Discretion prevents me from revealing the results of the day's event!)

A SPECIAL REQUEST FROM THE KING OF BASKETBALL

At the end of a fun fifty-four holes, we were cooling down from the heat of the day and visiting in the clubhouse. Michael leaned forward. "You know, Brad, I would do anything to have the opportunity to play golf with Arnold Palmer. He could tell me when and where … and I'm there! He's one of my all-time heroes. Even though he was close to the end of his competitive career when I was old enough to remember, I have watched most of the *Shell's Wonderful World of Golf*[4] competitions on the Golf Channel. I just loved his fearless and aggressive style as a competitor."

Frankly, I was taken aback. The greatest basketball player of all time was talking to me like a schoolboy about his desire to hang with the "King of golf," Arnold Palmer. Still serving in the capacity of host, I told Jordan that I was sure Mr. Palmer would be pleased to hear of his request and I promised to talk with him about it the next morning. Believe it or not, Jordan departed for the game at the Orlando Arena (after fifty-four holes of golf!), where he scored 18 points in a 153–113 thumping from the Western All-Stars.[5] I wonder if MJ overdid it with the golf.

I kept my promise. As I was passing through the grill room the next morning, I spotted Mr. Palmer sitting at his usual breakfast table, reading that morning's *Orlando Sentinel*. The front-page headlines were about Magic Johnson being awarded MVP of the previous evening's All-Star Game — Magic's first game since announcing his retirement.[6]

"Did you get a chance to watch that game last night?" I asked him. He said he had and he asked if I knew Michael Jordan had played golf at Bay Hill yesterday.

I chuckled. "I know!" I told him. "I was in his foursome with young Robert Damron. In fact, Jordan had a request for you."

Mr. Palmer put down his paper, intrigued.

"He wanted me to relay his gratitude for hosting him and said, 'Please tell Mr. Palmer that I would meet him anywhere, anytime — except during the final game of the playoffs — to play golf with him. He is one of my heroes and I would really like to have a chance to play a round with the King.'"

Arnold laughed heartily, a pleased grin sweeping across his face. "He said *that*?"

A MEETING FIT FOR KINGS

Arnie and Michael finally met and played at a Pro-Am Seniors Tournament at the Stonebridge Country Club in Illinois. How did they square off? Jordan, playing to an "eight" handicap, shot an estimated 36-45-81. The King started slowly, but he shot a 37-36-73 — just one over par.[7] What was Arnie's assessment of Jordan's golf game? "Michael swings the club very well and has a lot of potential," he said. "I was pleasantly surprised the way he goes after a golf ball. I enjoyed the game."[8]

I have in my library a little black book that I picked up at an airport and read in its entirety on a twenty-five-minute flight from Las Vegas to Rancho Cucamonga. The book is titled *I Can't Accept Not Trying*, with my favorite chapter being "Fear Is an Illusion." The author? Michael Jordan. I suggest that you add this book to your collection. Here is a brief excerpt:

> Sometimes failure actually just gets you closer to where you want to be. If I'm trying to fix a car, every time I try something that doesn't work, I'm getting closer to finding the answer. The greatest inventions in the world had hundreds of failures before the answers were found. I think fear sometimes comes from a lack of focus or concentration, especially in sports. If I had stood at the free throw line and thought about 10 million people watching me on the other side of

the camera lens, I couldn't have made anything. So I mentally tried to put myself in a familiar place.

I thought about all those times I shot free throws in practice and went through the same motion, the same technique that I had used thousands of times. You forget about the outcome. You know you are doing the right things. So you relax and perform. After that, you can't control anything anyway. It's out of your hands, so don't worry about it.

It's no different than making a presentation in the business world or doing a report for school. If you did all the things necessary, then it's out of your hands. Either the clients liked the presentation or they didn't. It's up to the client, the buyer, or the teacher. I can accept failure. Everyone fails at something. But I can't accept not trying. That's why I wasn't afraid to try baseball. I can't say, "Well, I can't do it because I'm afraid I may not make the team." That's not good enough for me. It doesn't matter if you win as long as you give everything in your heart and work at it 110 percent.[9]

Success is something you attract by the person you become.
MOTIVATIONAL SPEAKER AND AUTHOR
JIM ROHN

Arnold Palmer and Michael Jordan share a common perspective. From a competitive standpoint, these two spirits are one and the same. The fast friendship between the two is but one example that the best truly do attract the best. As the turn-of-the-century author Wallace Wattles wrote so eloquently, "To fix your attention on the best is to surround yourself with the best and to become the best."

For over fifty years, Arnold Palmer has made a habit of doing just that.

PART 3

Optimism Rules the Kingdom

The most rewarding things you can do in life are often the ones that look like they cannot be done.

ARNOLD PALMER

Is ANYONE BORN WITH an optimistic attitude? I'm reminded of the story of the little boy who didn't talk until he was seven years old. His parents were understandably worried. Doctors could find nothing wrong and were baffled. One morning the mother inadvertently served the son some cornflakes with sour milk. After one bite, the kid pushed the bowl back and hollered, "Yuck! No thank you, Mom!"

The mother was flabbergasted. "You can talk!" she exclaimed. As she hugged him, the mom said, "What happened? Why haven't you said anything for seven years?"

The boy replied, "Well, up until now, everything has been okay."

Even the most charmed life will have its ups and downs. Some people, like Arnold Palmer, are fortunate to have been raised and taught by parents to think and to expect positive results. But for many of us, soon after birth, our environment and experiences begin to condition us with certain expectations of what we can—and can't—achieve. This hinders many from reaching their full potential.

I see this daily in the attitude of many golfers who believe what they can and cannot achieve based on past outcomes and overall experiences. As a result, no matter what they try, they'll only rise to their preset level of expectation — and be disappointed. They console themselves with justifications of why they can't do something. They might say any one of the following:

"It's too hard."

"I'm just not talented enough."

"I don't have the time."

"It must be the ball ... or maybe the club."

"Playing with other people intimidates me."

"I just can't hit the ball far enough or straight enough."

"Why can't I finish my round without choking off a good score?"

> *A person's mental health has a greater effect on a person's success or failure than does any technique or opportunity.*

A person's mental health has a greater effect on a person's success or failure than does any technique or opportunity. In golf, technique is something many spend a lifetime trying to perfect, yet never become better players. Others, such as Arnold Palmer, take the time to develop a strong belief system whereby they know what they know and they don't fret and worry about what they don't know.

> *Attitude is a little thing that makes a big difference.*
> PRIME MINISTER WINSTON CHURCHILL

A study of success yields the observation that those who are truly triumphant in life have developed and nurtured an unfailing optimistic attitude as their chief companion. Those who have established and maintained a strong optimistic view have done it through conscious and deliberate effort. Though they don't always have a singular focus, they're constantly striving to keep their attention on what they want to achieve. They refuse to let disappointments define them; they refuse to believe they can't accomplish what they want to do. If these optimistic-minded people suffer a setback, they bounce back more determined and focused.

I have very little in common with the nineteenth-century German philosopher Friedrich Nietzsche. He was an atheist; I am a strong believer in the grace and goodness of my heavenly Father. But Nietzsche probably was right when he wrote, "What does not destroy me, makes me strong."[1]

Some people have this foolish impression that optimists are those with their heads in the clouds, living in denial of the world's troubles and disappointments. Truthfully, those of us who qualify ourselves as optimists are well aware of challenging times and circumstances. We've simply chosen to focus our energy toward doing something constructive. After all, as radio legend Paul Harvey often said, "I've never seen a monument erected to a pessimist."

Arnold Palmer is the consummate optimist. Even when all odds were against him — his 27-foot putt on the seventeenth hole and subsequent come-from-behind victory at the 1960 Masters, his remarkable seven-stroke comeback two months later at the U.S. Open, the dire diagnosis of prostate cancer — he refused to look at the glass as half empty. Regardless of the scenario or setback, he always kept the faith and refused to give up.

Most optimists I know believe in the sovereignty and majesty of God. Arnold Palmer has always believed in the mantra to work as if it were all up to him, but give thanks and praise as if it were all up to God. Palmer shared his thoughts and a simple prayer in *A Golfer's Life*. He wrote, "I've never been very superstitious, and my religious faith is more like my father's, a strictly private matter between my Maker and me. I did say prayers but never asked the Almighty to let me win a golf match or a tournament. My prayer was basically pretty simple and direct: 'Please let me stay healthy enough to compete.' Only injury or illness would keep me from being able to use my God-given physical abilities to win."[2]

This next portion of *Arnold Palmer's Success Lessons* will provide you with insight into how and where Arnold Palmer acquired and nurtured his spirit of optimism.

Go for Broke

My PERSONAL COPY OF Arnold Palmer's best-selling autobiography *Go for Broke: My Philosophy of Winning Golf*[1] is well worn, with dozens of dog-eared pages as proof of my personal endorsement. I've considered the book to be a staple, a handy resource that sums up Arnold Palmer's aggressive and unique approach to the game of golf. Sitting across from Arnie one day, I opened up its pages to one of my favorite quotes that he wrote almost forty years ago: "My test is always to go for broke—to try to win when common sense says it's all over."[2]

"You wrote that line four decades ago," I said, "at a time when you still had years of golf left in you. What does 'go for broke' mean to you now as you look back over your career and life?"

"I just went about playing golf the very best I could with all my focus on trying to win," Arnie said. "When you go for it, you will win some and also lose some. But I never looked at my losses as others did. I was disappointed but always felt like I learned something that was going to allow me to win next time I got into that same situation. 'Go for broke' for me is just that, putting it all on the line for a chance at victory. That was fun for me, exhilarating, and very gratifying as well."

AN EARLY INFLUENCE ON LETTING IT FLY

While he was still a teenager living in Latrobe, Arnie crossed paths with Babe Didrikson Zaharias, an early female sports superstar. Babe became known for her prowess in track and field, basketball, and, yes, golf — and Palmer, along with his father, Deacon, had the good fortune of playing a round with her. He remembers the day with great fondness.

"She was an extremely attractive lady and so nice. She talked to me like a buddy and a friend," Palmer remembered. "But she was also a great performer, and I'll never forget, she said, 'Arnie, I'm going to loosen up my girdle and let it fly.' And she did just that. She hit that ball farther than I could believe. At the time, I was very young in my golf and hadn't gotten to the point where I really knew what was going on, and I was very impressed with her. So that, coinciding with the things my father had been talking about, helped me model my career a little bit."[3]

Most golf historians point to Arnold's gutsy moves at the 1960 U.S. Open at Cherry Hills in Denver as the beginning of his tradition of aggressive play. For the first three rounds, he aggressively played the very tough first par-four hole — but with poor results. On Thursday he double-bogeyed the hole, he bogeyed it Friday, and during the first round on Saturday he finally parred it. Conventional wisdom would have dictated a conservative approach during the final round, but he went for it again — and birdied the hole. He would go on to birdie five of the next six holes and charged back to win the tournament. To this day, overcoming a seven-stroke deficit on the final day of play stands as the greatest comeback in U.S. Open history.[4]

But Palmer's penchant for aggressive play can actually be traced back to his high school play. In the state high school championship held at Penn State, Palmer recalls ignoring the advice of his high school friend caddie, who advised a cautious shot near the end of the final round. Instead of playing it safe, a young Arnie drilled his shot with a five iron over some trees. When asked why he didn't play it safe, he responded, "I didn't think that way. I saw the gap in the trees and thought, *That's a shot I think I can make*, so that's what I did. I guess I wasn't smart enough to do it any other way."[5] Interestingly, he can also vividly recall the approving roar of the crowd in the gallery that afternoon. It would become a sound he never grew tired of hearing.

THE BEAUTY OF BOLDNESS

I'm regularly inspired by the talks and writings of Dr. Norman Vincent Peale. For over fifty years, he served as the senior pastor of New York City's famed Marble Collegiate Church[6] and became known as the "father of positive thinking." But he wasn't always so chipper and optimistic about life. As a young boy and man, he suffered terribly from bouts of inferiority. When he assumed the pulpit of Marble Collegiate in 1932, the country was mired in the depths of the Great Depression. Only a few hundred people regularly showed up for services. The church was dying. Peale admitted to almost quitting several times—for several reasons—but he didn't. Instead, he launched an aggressive recruiting campaign for new members. He decided that if people wouldn't come to church, he'd go to the people.

Over the years, Peale accepted nearly every speaking invitation he was offered: the Lions Club, the Rotary Club, Boy Scouts, and others. It was a gutsy thing to do, being a pastor and wading into a clearly secular environment. He was also roundly criticized by fellow members of the clergy (for going soft), by intellectuals (for being too simplistic), and even by secularists (for being too religious). But he felt that he had something bold and effective to offer—the promise of the gospel—and he didn't shy from the open doors he was offered.

You might say Norman Vincent Peale was "going for broke," being bold and adventurous, taking a chance. I've always liked what he said on the subject of risk:

A certain degree of boldness is required of the individual who wishes to make more of himself. Boldness is an activator of power from the mind. As an author once said, "Go at it boldly, and you'll find unexpected forces closing round you and coming to your aid." The mind, ever the willing servant, will respond to boldness, for boldness, in effect, is a command to deliver mental resources. Boldly expect, and the power will come through.[7]

RISKS AND REWARDS

Arnold Palmer would cross paths with Peale through the years, and though they pursued very different lines of work, they clearly saw eye to eye on the benefits and risks of boldness. "The truth is my playing style caused me to lose as many majors as I won," Palmer admitted. "Did I behave irresponsibly? Not totally, because I had something in mind I wanted to do. Am I sorry for what I did? Yes, I am. Would I do it differently? Probably not. It's the way I was, and that's something I have to live with today."[8]

When taken in context, Arnold Palmer's admitted regrets are attributable to a mix of youthful exuberance and plain old inexperience. At the 1966 U.S. Open, he let slip a five-stroke lead with three holes to play and wound up losing a one-round playoff the next day too. When discussing his decades-long rivalry with Jack Nicklaus, Mr. Palmer said, "At times we became so hyper about beating each other that we let someone else go right by us and win. But our competition was fun and good for the game."

In 2000, the National Golf Foundation conducted a study examining what types of barriers and problems kept people from playing and continuing to play golf.[9] Interestingly, though game improvement was the focus of the study, researchers concluded that the fear of looking bad stops many high handicappers from taking lessons. Having been around golf courses my entire life, I know this is true, but I've never understood it. When I come across a duffer, I'm often tempted to say, "Look, you know you're a hacker. I know you're a hacker. I know you know you're a hacker. So why does it bother you that you know that I know that you know you are a hacker? Might be best to get over yourself, and let's get on with it!"

> *Show me a guy who is afraid to look bad and I will show you a man you can beat every time.*
> FORMER MAJOR LEAGUE BASEBALL PLAYER
> LOU BROCK

I regularly tell my clients (and myself) that "good shot or bad shot, it's all good as long as we grow from it." Self-awareness is necessary to learn from our mistakes. If we're fearful about looking bad in front of others, our mind will remain focused on what we don't want to happen.

> *If we're fearful about looking bad in front of others, our mind will remain focused on what we don't want to happen.*

THE LESSONS OF LEGENDS
Jack Nicklaus once said that embarrassment was one of his greatest motivators. Note that he said it was a motivator — not a deterrent. He told of a time, early in his career, when he double crossed a tee shot and pull hooked it left and out of bounds on the sixteenth hole of his final round. The error caused him to lose the event. He remembers telling himself, *I will never do that again!* After the tournament, he didn't make any excuses, nor did he become fearful of embarrassing himself again. He began practicing, repeatedly playing that same situation over and over

again in his mind. He convinced himself that the next time he found himself in that position, he was going to execute right down the middle of the fairway—and indeed he did just that.

Jack and Arnie are not afraid to put it on the line. In fact, doing so was a big part of the fun for them. They enjoyed the buzz of their hearts beating and experiencing the adrenaline rushing as they attempted to pull off a winning shot. One common difference that I have observed between the champion professionals and the rest is what happens after they finish their round of golf. The leaders will head to the practice tee to continue perfecting their game, while most golfers head directly to the nineteenth hole for a drink and a bite to eat. (In golf, the "nineteenth hole" is a term usually reserved for the bar at the club or course, but can be any drinking or dining establishment that golfers head to after eighteen holes.) This round of practice after a game might appear obsessive, but they're actually releasing the mistakes of the day and replacing them with the correct feelings of proper execution. At a time when the average golfer is commiserating with pals about that sliced tee shot on number eight or the missed putt on the final green, the pro is moving ahead of the problem, still going for broke.

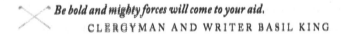

Be bold and mighty forces will come to your aid.
        CLERGYMAN AND WRITER BASIL KING

No matter what your game or dream, you can do the same.

Use Fear for Fuel

THE THOUGHT OF BEING motivated by fear seems to run contrary to what many of us have been taught to believe. Can fear ever be used to our advantage? Arnold Palmer not only believes that it can be used constructively, he also believes it's one of the main reasons for his success in golf over the course of these last fifty-plus years.

Are you skeptical? Fearful? You aren't alone. The legendary Christian writer J. R. R. Tolkien once suggested that fear was "bad for thinking."[1] New York Yankees owner George Steinbrenner, arguably the most controversial but successful executive in the history of baseball, was a man clearly driven to success by a fear of failure. George's father, Henry, was a world-class hurdler and used to run his boy through intense and demanding workouts in the family's backyard. George loved his father and worked tirelessly to make old Dad proud. One might question George Steinbrenner's intensity, but few would quibble with his success. He bought a deteriorating Yankees franchise for just over $8 million in 1973. At the time of his death in 2010, the Yankees had won an additional seven world championships and were estimated to be worth $1.6 billion. Most people, when faced with fear, retreat. George was ignited by the buzz to work smarter and harder toward his goal, his great love for success overcoming his fear of failure.

THE USE AND MANAGEMENT OF FEAR

In my personal library sits a prized possession—a thin black leather-bound book given to me by Mr. Palmer. It's titled *The Turning Point*,[2] and its contents are mostly Arnold Palmer's reflections of his matches and thoughts leading up to and throughout his 1954 U.S. Amateur Championship. I recently revisited this quick read, and it sparked my curiosity about Arnie's thoughts on his use and management of fear, especially when contrasted with the events of his early career that catapulted him to his next level of success.

"Mr. Palmer," I said, "I read in your book *The Turning Point* what your caddie Jimmy Gill said about you and your attitude during the week of the U.S. Amateur Championship. Gill was quoted as saying of you, 'He had something about him; that walk, the way he attacked the ball.' So let me ask you: Where do you think this inner confidence came from—all at the tender age of twenty-five?"

Arnold was quick to correct my error. "When I won the amateur, I was twenty-four," he stated, still smiling. "I was just short of coming up on twenty-five. And there were a lot of little things that made the difference in making it happen. One of the things that was very important was pretty simple: I didn't want to lose. I was afraid of losing! And I think that while everyone wants to win, not everybody is afraid to lose."

Up until then, despite all my years in golf, I'm not sure I'd ever thought about winning and losing in those terms. In effect, what Palmer was saying was that very few people are afraid to lose with the same degree of intensity as they have in wanting to win.

Very few people are afraid to lose with the same degree of intensity as they have in wanting to win.

"Everyone wants to win," Arnie said, "or they wouldn't do what they do. But not many people ever think about it. Many times I would think, *I can't lose. I just cannot.* Maybe it's an odd way to think, but it drove me to play harder than just 'thinking' about winning. Everybody wants to win the tournament, but this 'do or die' kind of outlook drove me to accomplish what I wanted and kept me moving forward. I made a lot of golf shots out of desperation, thinking that I had to pull it off because, frankly, I was afraid to lose."

It is better to be frightened now than killed hereafter.
PRIME MINISTER WINSTON CHURCHILL

DO-OR-DIE KIND OF GUY

I was eager to dive deeper into the origin of the mindset that triggered Arnie's do-or-die approach to golf. "How did you feel inside when you were going through those moments?" I asked. "For most people, that might generate crippling anxiety. But you were inspired to positive action and victory. How did you do it?"

Arnie inhaled deeply before responding. "It was an inspiration to me too that being a few shots behind inspired a 'must need' to hit the shots that I had to hit. And with this determination, I wiped out everything else from my thoughts. Of course, I think that was very positive for me. I didn't have any question in my mind that I could hit the shot I was trying to hit. People say, 'You really took a gamble!' But there was no gamble in my mind. I never thought it was a gamble to do what I did. Risky, yes; a gamble, no way! If I didn't pull it off, there were consequences, but I had confidence that I could pull off the shot that I had already pictured in my mind. To me, gambling would have been to try something that I didn't feel confident doing—or worse, not trying to pull it off and hoping that somehow it all was going to work out."

I would rather risk losing to win any day than lay up and hope for the best.

ARNOLD PALMER

Arnie was on a roll. "But that would mean the tournament was given to me instead of the fun of actually winning it!" he exclaimed. "And even though I have won this way before, those wins are never as sweet of a victory as those that you really go out and have to make happen through calculated risk. Putting the control into someone else's hands and not taking the action of being in control of the situation is much more of a gamble to me. I would rather risk losing to win any day than lay up and hope for the best."

THE DIFFERENCE BETWEEN RISKING AND GAMBLING

Whether I'm guiding my children or coaching my golf students, I've also tried to be clear on the critical difference between a "risk" and a "gamble." The term *gamble* is used to describe something that's more or less out of our hands and left to pure chance. On the other hand, a *risk* should be calculated, meaning that we've weighed the probability of success and deemed it worth our effort.

By that definition, Mr. Palmer was not a gambler, he was a man who took calculated risks. What type of person are you? Would it surprise you that too many people, in my estimation, are neither? Sadly, they play all of life ultrasafe and wind up missing out on some great adventures. Quitting your job to pursue a dream of running your own landscape business is not a gamble—unless you know absolutely nothing about cutting grass. Quitting your job and using your savings to buy scratch lottery tickets in the hope of striking it rich? Now that's a gamble!

I would urge you to consider living your life a bit more

aggressively. Don't be afraid to dream. Be bold. If I were an explorer and I knew what I wanted and I was prepared to set sail, I'd rather die at sea in a storm than spend the rest of my life tied up to a dock by the shore.

> *You get mentally tough through observing and emulating what other successful people do and putting yourself willingly into the heat of the battle, fighting to survive, and growing through each and every experience.*
>
> ARNOLD PALMER

THRIVING — NOT JUST SURVIVING

Arnold Palmer is a man who came of age during an era in America when the real heroes were those returning from World War II — and those who didn't. Arnold Palmer's America imposed and impressed good morals and a tough work ethic, and Palmer sought to emulate those who helped to lift this country from the grips of the Great Depression. There was an underlying philosophy that nothing good comes easy; it comes only through hard and consistent effort.

Robert Collier was born in 1885, a nephew of the founder of the famous *Collier's Weekly* publication. Collier became a popular writer of self-help books and once put into words the very thing that propelled Arnold Palmer to victory after victory: your greatest inspiration could very well be a fear of losing. Collier wrote:

> The mere fact that you have obstacles to overcome is in your favor, for when there is nothing to be done, when things run along too smoothly, this "Vital Force" seems to sleep. It is when you need it, when you call upon it urgently, that it is most on the job. It is the reserve strength of the athlete, the "second wind" of the runner, the power that, in moments of

great stress or excitement, you unconsciously call upon to do the deeds which you ever after look upon as superhuman.[3]

The reality of possibly losing what he really desired to achieve triggered in Palmer a motivation to dig deep and create the shots he desperately needed to win. To Arnold, success has always been the same as surviving, and he was courageous enough to use the emotion of fear to his advantage. It's true that Arnie took losses very personally. But it's critical to make a sharp distinction. For Mr. Palmer, honorable play was more important than victory. In other words, to be worthy of the win was just as crucial as the victory itself—if not more so.

The Power of Perseverance

ARNOLD PALMER HAS ALWAYS been a stickler for being on time. When it comes to keeping schedules and appointments with the King, the old adage of "better an hour early than a minute late" applies. On this particular day, we were scheduled for a quick trip from Orlando to the first round of the Tournament Players Club (TPC) in Tampa Bay, Florida.[1] I had been advised we'd be "wheels in the well" by 6:30 a.m. ("Wheels in the well" is Palmer's code for advising when he wants us to be in the air, i.e., the time when the landing gear better be up and locked away in the belly of the plane.) I knew better than to be late.

The privilege of flying on the King's Cessna Citation X (which at the time of writing was the fastest civilian aircraft in the world, capable of breaking the speed of sound) never gets old. When I boarded the jet that morning, Arnold had already jumped into the pilot's seat and was going through the preflight checklist. Though he always flies with his trusted copilot, Pete Luster, Palmer began flying in the 1950s and has logged well over 18,000 miles of flight hours.[2]

It was an extremely short flight of twenty minutes, and as we pulled into the Tampa Municipal Airport terminal, I heard him talking to Pete. Arnie sounded like he was struggling mightily with a head cold. When he came out of the cockpit to say "Hello" and "Good morning," it was obvious to me that the man was miserable. He was squinting through his watery eyes and speaking with a frog-like tenor voice. He looked like he should have stayed home in bed for the day.

WATCHING THE STAR ON A DIFFERENT STAGE

Over the next several hours, I would observe one of the King's most incredible performances—but this time it had little to do with his swing and everything to do with intestinal fortitude. Arnold is nearly obsessive when it comes to keeping his obligations; if he agrees to do something, it's almost as good as being done. That day was no different. Palmer had promised he would attend and play in the tournament—people were expecting him there—and Arnold would not disappoint his fans.

> *When you are tough on yourself, life is going to be infinitely easier on you.*
>
> MOTIVATIONAL SPEAKER AND AUTHOR
> ZIG ZIGLAR

As soon as the courtesy car rolled into the players' parking lot and word got out that Arnie was on the property, a buzz rippled through the crowds waiting there. I spotted a large throng of people hustling our way. Members of the media, everyday fans, and tournament sponsors all wanted a moment with the "King of golf." As he made his way from the locker room to the practice fairway for his pre-round warm-up, he stopped and visited, shook hands, and posed for photographs with his fans.

From my vantage point, Arnie appeared to have made a miraculous recovery. He had a broad smile on his face. He was standing tall and acting energized. He looked like a million bucks. From every indication, he was giving his very best to each interaction. Even more importantly, Arnold genuinely appeared to be enjoying himself—and because he was happy, everyone around him was happy too.

Throughout the course of his round, out of sight of the cameras and the fans, I would occasionally catch a glimpse of Arnold inconspicuously taking a few deep breaths and resting heavily on his bag. Only Arnold's caddie, Royce; his pilot, Pete; and I knew that Mr. Palmer was doing his best just to make it through the day. There was no doubt he was struggling, but he never once talked about it or tried to gain sympathy. When it was his turn to go, and cameras and lights came back on, Arnie was onstage and a hundred percent focused on the shot or the conversation at hand. As I recall, Mr. Palmer finished the day with a respectable score of one under par and just four shots off the lead.

THE LESSON OF THE DAY

Looking back on that day in Tampa, I realized what a magnificent acting job had taken place. For Palmer, it was truly an example of mind over matter. When Arnold and entourage climbed back into the courtesy car and headed for the airport, he was incredibly congested and hoarse. If I were a star in my seventies with ninety-two Tour victories and more than enough money to pay for groceries, would I have persevered in similar fashion? Would you?

In the days since, I've thought about that experience, especially when I am not feeling my best and inclined to blow off the day. In doing so, I'm reminded of the role I play in other people's lives and how they might be affected or inconvenienced by my absence. The quirky comedian and film star Woody Allen once wryly observed that "eighty percent of success is showing up."[3] I think Woody's math is a bit subjective, but the overall premise is correct.

MAKING IT PERSONAL

When the twenty-five-year-old Palmer married twenty-year-old Winifred Walzer on December 24, 1954, he was a rising star, a professional for just over a month. One of the first decisions he made was to make sure that Winnie traveled with him on the tour. He enjoyed the closeness and the chance for Winnie to live within his world. Their daughter Peg was born on February 26, 1956. Amy arrived two years later on August 4, 1958. During those early years with the girls, the family often traveled together, carting all of the necessary baby paraphernalia from one city to the next.

All because Arnie believed strongly in the principle of "showing up" for the family. All because he wanted to be around so he'd be involved in their lives and they in his. When the girls reached school age, Winnie, Peg, and Amy (until summer break) remained in Latrobe, while Daddy continued to dominate golf around the world. It was tough being separated for weeks on end, but the reunion was always a joyful celebration loaded with hours of show-and-tell. Palmer did his best to balance the importance of family with his growing global business obligations. Sometimes it took his trusting soul mate to remind him when business had begun to consume their family time. Winnie and Arnold also did their best to raise the girls like normal little girls, trying to send them to public schools so that they wouldn't feel different from other kids. Remaining grounded is a key ingredient to "showing up" in the Palmer family. That is how they all roll, even today, thanks to the good example handed down to the next generation.

As the father of four wonderful children—Bradley, Tori, Carli, and Kenna—I can relate to what Mr. Palmer has done to find and cultivate time with his family. Today, I'm fortunate that my wife, Wanda, and I run our own business and plot and plan our own hours. But everything comes with a price. There have been plenty of times when I easily could have taken on a few more clients and made additional income — but only at the expense of the kids and my wife.

Whatever it is you might be doing, it's a matter of balance and moderation. The key to making good decisions is knowing what you care about most. Because if you know what you care about, you'll inevitably know how to act.

Arnold Palmer has made a career of showing up — but he's beloved for more reasons than his perfect attendance record. He is a disciplined performer who diligently works to feed and maintain a positive mindset, a trait that allows him to dip deeply into his vast reserves and pull off what his body would otherwise not allow him to do.

The idea of "faking it till you make it" is not a principle borne out of disingenuousness or insincerity. Rather it's a habit of the head and a practice of sometimes doing the hard thing for all the right reasons. It's giving of yourself for the sake of others. It's putting the greater good ahead of personal convenience and comfort.

Turn Adversity to Your Advantage

In January of 1997, at the age of sixty-seven, Arnold Palmer was diagnosed with prostate cancer.[1] In typical Palmer fashion, he received the news, consulted with experts, and chose to pursue an aggressive form of treatment. Fortunately, the news was promising; the cancer was caught early and he underwent surgery, followed by several rounds of radiation.

Successful golfers have an innate ability to keep an optimistic viewpoint and bounce back quickly from a double bogey and get focused on making birdies again. Comparing his challenge with cancer to a tough shot on the golf course, the King reflected, "You have a couple of options. You can play it out with a wedge and then hit another shot to the green. Or you hit it between the trees and get it done right then and there and have no other shot to worry about. I didn't want to be walking around thinking I could still have cancer. That's the reason I chose surgery."[2]

We all breathed a sigh of relief when, several months later, the Mayo Clinic reported to Arnie that he was officially cancer free. Most people would have been elated, but instead of walking away from the burdens and challenges that accompany cancer, Arnie found in the experience a new mission and calling in life.

RAISING AWARENESS

Following his bout with cancer, Arnold was delighted to become a spokesman for prostate cancer awareness, urging men to tackle the disease through early detection. With his support, a massive public health awareness campaign was launched. For over ten years, the Prostate Cancer Foundation has partnered with Arnold Palmer and Arnie's Army to raise money for prostate cancer research by holding annual celebrity golf tournaments. These one-day events are built around a closest-to-the-pin contest on a par three hole. Banners, posters, pin flags, and other materials carry the program logo, and all golfers are encouraged to join Arnie's Army to help win the battle against prostate cancer.

The efforts of Arnie's Army have been wildly successful. Beginning in 2002, the nonprofit organization has been moving across the nation with a goal of enlisting hundreds of thousands and raising several million dollars for the Prostate Cancer Foundation's mission. To date, Arnie's Army has sponsored 1,300 events, raising more than $1.5 million in the fight against prostate cancer.[3]

"Most of us would rather not discuss cancer because we are all afraid we might be told we have it," Palmer has said. "It's hard for people to even say the word, and that's the first obstacle you have to overcome when you are diagnosed with the disease. I don't mean it gets any easier, but I think you give it more in-depth thought about how you're going to deal with it."[4]

TURNING LEMONS INTO LEMONADE

I recently heard a story that struck me as a good lesson on how to approach struggles. In the late 1790s, the common belief throughout the Australian colony was that the region beyond the imposing Blue Mountains was lush and fertile—but inaccessible. Afraid of the steep ridges and deep gorges, explorers followed the more inviting routes, such as rivers and gently rolling paths. But each attempt was met with failure.

By 1813, the colony was gripped in the stranglehold of an awful drought. With their food supply dwindling, the governor and his people were desperate. If only they could get to the other side of the Blue Mountains, they'd have access to the arable fields they needed to survive.

You've heard the saying that desperate times call for desperate measures? Three men—Gregory Blaxland, William Lawson, and William Wentworth—felt just that way. They decided to do the "impossible" and cross the mountains by following the rough and jagged ridges. In other words, instead of going *around* the mountains, they decided to go *over* them.

The unorthodox approach was successful. A new pathway was established, resources were procured, and the colony began to grow with great gusto.

I believe there's a parallel to our struggles today. The easiest route to a solution isn't always the best. And with risk there often comes a reward. Are you facing a difficult problem today? Are you trying to solve an "impossible" or "insurmountable" challenge? Maybe the answer to your "insurmountable" problem is to do the difficult thing and take the hard way.

Of course, with Arnold's cancer diagnosis, he didn't really have a choice. Or did he? How often do we face the challenges of life from a negative point of view? Sometimes I think we view our circumstances akin to a fate that has simply fallen upon us.

Only God can heal—but we can certainly do our part by approaching our problems with a proactive and positive attitude.

GOD'S PERFECT PLAN

Has it ever occurred to you that if God is really in complete control, then we have nothing to worry or fret about? This might strike you as strange, but sometimes the very worst thing that could happen to us is the very best thing for us — depending upon God's ultimate plan.

I've witnessed the generosity of Mr. Palmer for years. But I wonder how his charitable giving might have differed had he not been personally impacted by cancer. I share with you in his words:

> August 23, 1989, is a day I'll never forget. Thousands were on hand for the opening and dedication of the Arnold Palmer Hospital for Children. There was a host of young entertainers and singing characters from Disney World, a marching band, various area dignitaries and friends, and the press.
>
> It was just before my sixtieth birthday, and I guess I was in a pretty reflective mood. The hospital project had grown to mean so much to both Winnie and me and our family — the ultimate pet project in some ways. As speeches were made and thousands of balloons were released, I was feeling fine and in control. That is, until six-year-old Billy Gillespie, a new patient at the facility, held the microphone and spoke to the gathering — and to me personally. Billy thanked me for making a "dream come true."
>
> I remember glancing at my daughter Amy, with her husband, Roy, and her four healthy children gathered around her, and feeling a knot of gratitude tighten my throat and chest. Though we couldn't possibly have known it then, Amy would soon go through her own ordeal with cancer — and come out on the other side, wiser and healed, thanks to a world-class treatment center like the hospital we had just helped create. When I saw the tears of pride and thanks forming in Amy's eyes, that's when I lost it.
>
> Once again, I was crying in public.

Arnold Palmer has made a career of making the best out of

tough lies. He's shown me that being able to deal with life's daily challenges and struggles with an optimistic approach will allow us to find the silver lining of even the darkest cloud.

> *When we are no longer able to change a situation, we are challenged to change ourselves.*
> AUSTRIAN NEUROLOGIST, PSYCHIATRIST,
> AND HOLOCAUST SURVIVOR
> VIKTOR FRANKL

Ironically, a drink commonly known as an "Arnold Palmer"[5] consists of mixing a half glass of unsweetened iced tea with a half glass of lemonade. Quite fitting, isn't it, given the man's proclivity and ability to turn something tart into something sweet.

Compliment and Encourage

ARNOLD PALMER'S GOOD FRIEND PGA veteran Peter Jacobsen is certainly no stranger to success. Since turning pro in 1977, this Oregon native has taken home seven titles on the PGA Tour and won on the Champions Tour twice.[1] He's also just a fun and interesting guy to hang around with. A self-taught guitarist, Pete has jammed onstage with such legendary performers as Huey Lewis and the News, Hootie & the Blowfish, and REO Speedwagon. Believe it or not, he's also one of the few golfers to have formed a band. Pete and fellow golfers Mark Lye and Payne Stewart created and launched Jake Trout and the Flounders in the mid-1980s.[2] Once called "the Johnny Carson of golf," he and his partners would write humorous golf-themed lyrics to popular songs and perform them at golfing events around the country. Take his rendition of "Struggler's Blues,"[3] sung to the tune of "Smuggler's Blues" by Glenn Frey:

> I knew that there'd be trouble, trouble here today,
> Anxiety's building and it wouldn't go away.
> Always try to fight it but that target's looking small,
> Got a funny feeling that I'm gonna miss 'em all.
> I got a lot of questions, I'd love to find out why,
> Got to make some sense of this someday before I die.
> Bring some relief to this damaged sense of pride,
> I can't believe I'm into this,

I really hate to lose.
Asking forgiveness,
Got the Struggler's Blues ... Struggler's Blues.

If you'd like to read more about some of his comical perspectives, I'd recommend you pick up his latest book, *Embedded Balls: Adventures On and Off the Tour with Golf's Premier Storyteller.*[4] His first book back in 1993 was equally funny: *Buried Lies: True Tales and Tall Stories from the PGA Tour.*[5]

> *Pleasant words are a honeycomb, sweet to the soul and healing to the bones.*
>
> KING SOLOMON, PROVERBS 16:24

Peter Jacobsen is a colorful character and a big-hearted man. He has a gift for taking himself and life lightly, but when it comes to the appreciation he holds for Arnold Palmer—including his habit of crediting the King for helping to launch his career—Jacobsen turns deadly serious. I've invited Pete to share his thoughts on his friend and mentor, Arnold Palmer. As you read the following essay, I suspect you'll be struck, as I was, by just how simple, powerful, and effective a compliment and a few words of encouragement can be for a young athlete.

A COMPLIMENT FROM THE KING
Peter Jacobsen

When I was ten years old, my mom was very involved with the PGA Tour event in Portland, Oregon. At the time, I enjoyed playing all sports, but especially golf, and that particular year the Tour featured Dave Marr and the "King of golf," Arnold Palmer. The two were conducting a Junior Golf Clinic on the Tuesday before the event, so I, along with a couple hundred other kids, went to watch and learn from two of my idols.

Dave Marr really impressed me as a strong ball striker and seemed able to place the ball wherever he wanted. His swing was smooth and effortless. Then Palmer got up and started hitting drivers, and you could almost hear the ground shake. He really smacked that ball! To a little kid, Arnold Palmer was bigger than life. He was like watching a gun slinger swagger onto the driving range with muscles and Hollywood movie star looks.

To my great delight and thrill, Palmer and Marr invited me to participate in the clinic. I went up in front of the crowd—I was really nervous—and, at least for me, managed to hit some pretty good shots. But as fun as the experience was, forty years later, one thing in particular stands out in my memory.

Both men, but especially Arnie, were incredibly complimentary and offered powerful words of encouragement about the strength of my swing and overall golfing ability. It made me feel like a million bucks! It didn't just put a smile on my face or boost my self-esteem; it sparked my interest in putting more effort into my golf game.

I have no doubt that the positive reaction from Arnold Palmer infused me with a level of confidence I had never before experienced. Shortly after attending that clinic, I began playing in tournaments. I've never stopped. When a few small wins began to accumulate, I can remember thinking to myself, *Wow, you can make money doing this?* Well, that was almost forty years ago, and I have enjoyed a pretty good life doing exactly that.

When I came on Tour in 1977, I reminded Arnold of our first exchange and of just how important it was to me. He seemed pleased and smiled, but quickly turned the tables back on me. "Good!" he said. "But, Pete, now make sure that you don't forget to return the favor when you're given the chance to encourage young and aspiring players."

Fortunately, that day has come. I've been given the privilege of conducting the Junior Clinics on the PGA Tour throughout many weeks during the year. And you can be sure that I try to do the same thing that Dave Marr and Arnold Palmer did for me: encouraging the boys and girls that we have a chance to meet. I learned a long time ago that compliments with everyone go a very long way—but especially so with juniors. Kids are like sponges! When you're paying attention to them and offering encouraging words, they're bound to fill up with pride and confidence, exactly like I did a few years ago.

Well, okay, maybe it's been more than just a few.

I can live for two months on a good compliment.
AUTHOR AND HUMORIST MARK TWAIN

Robert H. Schuller, the founding pastor of the Crystal Cathedral in California, has been serving up inspirational sermons for over fifty years. My mother and father first introduced me to Schuller's television program back when I was just a young boy. He is deft at turning a phrase and boosting a downtrodden spirit. With a flair for the dramatic (he considered Fulton Sheen and Norman Vincent Peale to be his mentors), he would say such things as, "Tough times don't last, but tough people do!" Or "It takes guts to get out of the ruts!" But when it came to encouraging young people to pursue the dreams that God has laid on their hearts, Schuller was even more direct: "Build a dream, and the dream will build you!"

Thanks to the encouraging words of Arnold Palmer, Peter Jacobsen began to build his dream, and his dream built him into the man he is today.

Believe in Yourself

No MATTER HOW MANY TIMES I've had the pleasure of visiting Arnie's Latrobe office, the golf junkie in me never tires of looking at the hundreds upon hundreds, if not thousands, of pieces of golf memorabilia in and around the vast Pennsylvania complex. There are walls of photographs of the King with presidents: Eisenhower, Kennedy, Johnson, Nixon, Ford, Carter, Reagan, George H. W. Bush, Bill Clinton, and George W. Bush (the picture with George W. Bush features Palmer receiving the Presidential Medal of Freedom in 2004). The most recent presidential photo features President Barack Obama awarding Palmer the Congressional Gold Medal, the highest civilian honor for distinguished achievements and contributions. The last and only other golfer to be awarded that particular medal was Byron Nelson in 2006.[1]

Friends like to joke with Palmer about his being both a member of sports royalty—and so old he probably played a few rounds with George Washington. "I didn't know George Washington," Palmer deadpans, "but if I did, I would shake his hand and say, 'You're the first, and won't be the last.'"[2]

HUMILITY IN SECURITY

The English writer and Christian apologist G. K. Chesterton once wrote, "It is always the secure who are humble," and it's clear to me, after looking at Arnie's awards and contrasting them with his quiet spirit, that he is about as secure as they come. I've always been intrigued by this. How does such a big man grow so comfortable in his own skin? How was he able to maintain a strong sense of self-confidence—something that's necessary to win—but not become an egomaniac in the process?

A man wrapped up in himself makes for a very small bundle.
BENJAMIN FRANKLIN

I once asked him, "This strong sense of self-confidence is a big part of your success. Trusting in your own ability to pull off so many key shots at just the right time led you to many championships. You were aggressive but not cocky. How did you pull this off?"

"Well, Brad," he began, "I diligently focused on what I desired and worked hard at getting a little better every day, sharpening my strengths and also focusing on the areas in my game that needed improvement. I believe that with each good performance, my successes increased my confidence and awareness regarding what I needed to do to win. With every win, I began to trust and believe in my ability to win again. This allowed me to think more about expanding my goals and what I wanted most of all: to keep on improving and win more golf tournaments."

But how did he keep his head on straight? How did he maintain humility, especially when the wins and prizes came early and often?

"Earlier in my career," he said, "my father, Deacon, would remind me to stay grounded. He would tell me to remember where I came from, to keep my feet on the ground, and to focus on my work and not get too caught up with all of the accomplishments. I can remember coming back from winning the British

Open in 1961, where I was dining with dukes and princes over the course of an entire week. I came home to Latrobe, excited about my victory. My dad greeted me with open arms and, with his second breath, said, 'Now, why don't you put down that claret jug. I need your help mowing the back nine.' Looking back, this was a very important marker to me. It reminded me that if I'm going to be successful, I must continue to grow with a balance of confidence and humble appreciation for all the people involved in making it possible."

The average golfer will often struggle when it comes to confidence; we tend to be very fickle creatures. For many of us, we're only as good—or as bad—as our last golf shot. My clients tend to be very hard on themselves, always afraid of looking bad or being embarrassed. They may begin the day with an optimistic outlook, but they quickly find themselves obsessing over missed shots and opportunities. Self-defeated and wondering why last week's grip lesson and their brand-new driver stopped working as well as they did on the driving range, they often spiral into frustration and despair.

It ain't what they call you; it's what you answer to.
                                                      W. C. FIELDS

WHAT DO YOU EXPECT OF YOURSELF?

Arnold Palmer's eternally optimistic approach to playing golf certainly contributed to his ability to win more than ninety-two times as a professional golfer. His "go for broke" philosophy allowed him to play aggressively, without regrets and second-guessing. He deliberately emptied and cleared his mind of self-doubt and mistrust. It's been argued that Palmer was pragmatic in his approach. I don't agree. Certainly his disciplined thoughts were a guide to his actions. But what inspired his thoughts was a belief in his own ability to perform and to win. He always anticipated the best possible outcome because he believed he was equipped with the best possible skills and habits of the game.

Basketball great Michael Jordan once said, "You have to expect things of yourself before you can do them." That's exactly right! Like his friend MJ, Arnold Palmer has lived a life of high personal expectations. As I will often tell my clients and friends when summing up my opinion of why Palmer has consistently succeeded where others have failed, he is the King who truly rules his own kingdom — the six inches between his ears!

PART 4

HEROES IN ACTION

You must play boldly to win.... Always make a total effort
even when the odds are against you.

ARNOLD PALMER

NEVER GIVE UP!

You've probably heard the story of how Thomas Edison failed more than two thousand times in his attempt to invent the electric lightbulb. Then, on December 9, 1914, the great inventor's New Jersey laboratory caught on fire. Standing in the glow of the flames, he excitedly said to his son, "Charles, go get your mother. She will never see another fire like this one!"[1] He suffered over $7 million in property damage.[2] What was his response to the great catastrophe? "There is great value in disaster," he was reported to have said the next morning. "All our mistakes are burned up. Thank God we can start anew."[3] At the age of sixty-seven, Thomas Edison rebuilt his empire and lived and worked another seventeen years before his death in 1931.

Edison once remarked thoughtfully, "Many of life's failures are people who did not realize how close they were to success when they gave up."

Like Edison, Arnold Palmer never let failure keep him down. He may have lost hundreds of tournaments, but he's defined by his victories, not the defeats. Part of the reason for this is that he possesses what I refer to as a hero's heart and soul. I've always admired Arnie's skillful way of thinking clearly and quickly, creating successful opportunities out of challenges and great difficulties. Like Edison, he never let a setback prevent him from embarking on a comeback.

This next section of *Arnold Palmer's Success Lessons* focuses on how Arnold Palmer's aggressive philosophy toward the game of golf and the world of business regularly moved him toward his desired outcome. It also gave him the courage to take action and make timely decisions with confidence. Whether in golf or business, Arnold Palmer has been able to hit what some people call the "terror barrier" and bust through it with focus, conviction, and faith. So we'll examine the importance of taking ownership for the failure or the success of your actions, for Arnie's mindset is simple: failure or success is all good as long as you can learn from your failures and continue moving forward.

Turn Negatives into Positives

THE SOUTHERN HILLS COUNTRY CLUB in suburban Tulsa is one of the most beautiful courses in America. There is a quiet dignity and charm to the legendary property, from its white clubhouse framed by towering elm trees to its slowly moving creeks and green rolling hills. All the legends of golf have played the old course, from Hogan to Sneed to Woods, but for Arnold Palmer, it's the site of one of the most disappointing losses of his career.

It was August 1970. At the time, the PGA Championship had long eluded the King, and he was determined to end the drought. Despite the fact that he had been the only golfer to have played all forty rounds of Firestone tournaments in the 1960s, he decided to skip a big tournament in Akron, Ohio, the week prior in order to rest up.

By all accounts, Arnie played well that weekend, always lurking within a few shots of the lead. But in the end, he couldn't pull it off. He tied for second, losing to Dave Stockton by two strokes. He would never again come so close to winning the PGA Championship.

It's hard to see the upside to failure, but during that weekend in Tulsa, there was an incredible moment to remember. At one point of the tournament, Mr. Palmer found himself in the trees, approximately 150 yards away from the pin. He had no shot at the green, really, and everyone there assumed he would simply chip his shot up onto the fairway and prepare for a better approach. The spectators grew curious, however, as Arnie began taking an unusually long time to set up. Finally, he took his swing and sent the ball sailing right through a tiny opening in the trees. And wouldn't you know—the ball landed smack dab on the green!

For those in attendance that day, that one moment summed up Arnold Palmer's approach to golf. It's true you can't win every tournament, and even the King of golf may come up short—like never winning a PGA Championship. But the key is to engage and try to find the upside to a challenging situation. Or, in this case, find the tiny opening in a grove of thick, leafy elm trees.

"It's true that I went for it often and it didn't always work," Palmer told me. "That's obvious by my record and by the things that happened."

It may sound like a cliché to say that "winning isn't everything," but the King inevitably and invariably found something positive out of every otherwise negative or losing golf performance. "The enjoyment that I got out of 'going for it' and trying to make it work was very rewarding to me personally," he said. "A lot of people think that the tournaments I lost as a result of aggressive play were a real downer for me. They weren't. The experience was all just a continuation of the things I felt I had to do personally. And the fact was that I went for broke a lot of times—and a lot of times it worked out and I won!"

I share Arnie's mindset—focusing on the possibilities before him—but a lot of people have a difficult time seeing the silver lining of a dark cloud. They accuse optimists of subscribing to a Pollyanna perspective—a sweet idea, but very unrealistic.

"I know," Palmer told me, "there were times when I went for it and it just didn't work. But it *wasn't* a downer. It was actually more of an enlightenment to me. Some of it *was* negative, but I didn't create or feel like I was creating a negative situation. I think I was learning by what I was doing, turning a negative into a positive. And in doing so, it often inspired me to work harder so that the next time, I was confident and ready to go for it and win."

> *I've missed more than nine thousand shots in my career. I've lost more than three hundred games. I've been trusted to take the game-winning shot and missed. I've failed over and over and over again in my life, and that is why I succeed.*
>
> BASKETBALL LEGEND MICHAEL JORDAN

TAKING OUR CHALLENGES TO HEART

When faced with obstacles or expected defeat, too many of us can find the slightest excuse to give up or give in—especially after enduring a gut-wrenching loss. Someone once asked me if I knew of a place where there were thousands upon thousands of people without a care or problem in the world. Where could this place possibly be? A lush tropical island? The estate of a billionaire? Hardly. It was the local cemetery, the person told me. Translation: If you're alive, you'll have problems. In fact, it's been said that the more problems you have, the more alive you are!

Norman Vincent Peale once wrote:

We will all have difficulties at some point in our lives. What matters is how we handle them. And what we do with them depends upon whether we know the power we have over them. The believer is conferred power over difficulties. In the twenty-first chapter of Matthew we read: "Jesus said to them, 'If you have faith and don't doubt, I promise that you can do what I did to this tree. And you will be able to do even more. You can tell this mountain to get up and jump into the sea, and it will. If you have faith when you pray, you will be given whatever you ask for.'"[1]

FAILURE IS NEVER FINAL

British writer J. R. R. Tolkien, an Oxford professor, is perhaps best known for authoring *The Hobbit*[2] and *The Lord of the Rings*.[3] At one point in his career, Tolkien coined the word *eucatastrophe*, a term he created by affixing the Greek prefix *eu*, meaning "good," to *catastrophe*.[4] In essence, Tolkien was attempting to find a term to describe those situations in life when something very bad suddenly turns very good. He considered the crucifixion and resurrection of Jesus Christ to be the ultimate eucatastrophe. Why? Consider: Here was a man led away to be killed on a cross. All his friends had abandoned him, and it appeared that even his heavenly Father had done the same. His hour finally came and the sky turned black. He died an excruciating death. By sundown, all hope seemed loss. Three years of ministry and miracles were history. But suddenly, Sunday morning came. The tomb was empty! And everything turned out just as he (Jesus) said it would. This is why even the "worst" day of the Christian calendar—the day Jesus was crucified—is now called "*Good* Friday."

I am not attempting to equate the fortunes of golf to the life of Jesus Christ. But the idea that bad things can actually turn out to be very good things is the very point of this lesson. Christ's weakness turned out to be his strength, and the certain defeat became the greatest victory in all the world. Has it ever occurred to you that the very worst things that happen to you could wind up sowing the seeds to your greatest success?

TURNING BAD EXPERIENCE INTO GOOD OPPORTUNITIES

In 1951, Charles Kemmons Wilson was enjoying moderate success as a real-estate developer. Married with five children, the Wilsons had a comfortable middle-class life in Memphis. They decided to take a vacation and drove across the country, staying at cheap motels along the way. Accommodations were lousy. Wilson grew increasingly irritated at the inconsistent service and the extra fees. "My six-dollar room became a $16, or my eight-dollar room became $18," Wilson remembered. "I told my wife, Dorothy, that wasn't fair. I didn't take many vacations, but as I took this one, I realized how many families there were taking vacations and how they needed a nice place they could stay."[5]

Instead of complaining and letting the memories of a bad vacation linger, Wilson opened a small hotel with a dream of opening many more all across the country and helping families avoid having the same bad experience. Today, Holiday Inn is a worldwide hotel chain owned by the InterContinental Hotels Group.[6]

Pastor and author Adrian Rogers once remarked that "the door to the room of opportunity swings on the hinges of opposition."[7] Charles Wilson would agree, and so would Arnold Palmer, who doesn't just work harder than most; he's also learned how to turn negatives into positives.

Win or lose, it's all good as long as you grow from it.

When I was young, I observed that nine out of every ten things I did were failures, so I did ten times more work.

IRISH PLAYWRIGHT
GEORGE BERNARD SHAW

Pressure Produces Results

ARNOLD PALMER GREW UP in the warm glow of the nearby United States Steel Corporation. Founded in 1901, the Pittsburgh-based company has had ties with such notable and illustrious capitalist magnates as Andrew Carnegie, J. P. Morgan, and Charles Schwab.[1] Being so close to the hub of steel-making, Arnie learned a valuable lesson at a very early age: the best way to forge steel is the old-fashioned Pittsburgh way—with the heat of a raging red-hot furnace. Perhaps unknowingly, Palmer has carried this same philosophy into both his golf and his business dealings.

My boss seems to thrive under pressure; in fact, he clearly enjoys pressure. But that's not all. The King also enjoys challenging his colleagues and associates to raise their game and take it to the next level. Arnold Palmer believes pressure produces positive results.

PUT ON THE SPOT

When I was still a rookie with the Palmer group and struggling mightily to keep up with Arnie's warp-speed daily routine, I was invited to attend a key presentation in Rancho Cucamonga, California, where we were opening a beautiful new course at the foot of the San Gabriel Mountains. This special gathering would be comprised of high-level executives, investors, and journalists. Since an academy would be opening on site there at the

Empire Lakes Golf Course, I was to be on hand to answer any questions.

As luck would have it, both of my flights were delayed, and I was forced to arrive late, with the press conference already in progress. I quickly hopped out of my taxi and scurried for the conference room with my bags in tow. As soon as I found the correct room, I swung open the door, making a scene by interrupting the mayor, already at the podium before an entire room of city dignitaries, the General Dynamics executives who owned the property, and a significant number of the Los Angeles press corps. They all turned in unison to see what the Santa Ana winds had blown in.

I was mortified. My delay was unavoidable, but my grand entrance was a good way to make a bad first impression. Slinking into the room, I made eye contact with Arnold. He was sitting up front, right next to the podium with Ed Seay, his design partner. There was an empty chair on the dais, and Arnie motioned to me to take it. To make matters worse, I noticed that everyone—including Arnold Palmer—was in a coat and tie. The memo on the dress code must never have reached me, and I was clad in khakis and a casual polo shirt. *Ouch!* Settling into my high-profile seat, I could practically feel heat coming off my rosy red cheeks. You could have fried an egg on 'em.

STEPPING UP

The standard procedure at such events usually calls for Arnold and Ed to do the talking. I'm always introduced, but all I need to do is stand and be recognized, smile, and sit back down. But without warning, the King strode to the microphone and made a startling announcement—shocking, at least, to me. Throwing a wink and a smile my way, Arnie announced, "And now I will turn the rest of this presentation over to our academy director to tell you about the soon-to-open Arnold Palmer Golf Academy."

When we long for life without difficulties, remind us that oaks grow strong in contrary winds and diamonds are made under pressure.

PREACHER PETER MARSHALL

Shell-shocked, but still vertical, I stepped to the podium, passing my boss on the way. Arnie leaned over and whispered in my ear, "You're late!"

I quickly sized up three things: the room, the challenge, and the opportunity. I took a deep breath and, suddenly, something triggered inside me. It was time to show Arnold what I could do! Before launching into the presentation, I quickly uttered a silent prayer. Reaching down to recall the specifics of the material I had been working on for the past fourteen months, I was almost shocked to hear the polished words that came from my mouth. After thirty minutes of presentation and Q&A, I stepped down and again walked past Mr. Palmer. He again whispered in my ear. "You are forgiven, and nice job!"

PEOPLE RISE TO THE OCCASION

Thankfully, I passed the acid test that day and, in Palmer's eyes, proved my worth to his corporation. His trust and confidence in my ability to represent his brand in the marketplace began to grow. But looking back, thanks to Palmer putting me under pressure, I was forced to do something I had not done prior to that presentation. He gave me an opportunity to show my worth, and I rose to the challenge.

My experience, both in business and in my personal life—especially parenting kids—is that when people are put under some degree of strain and expectation, they will usually rise to the occasion. The same is true for you. Unless you're woefully unqualified or unprepared, you will almost always meet the demand.

> *Pressure is a word that is misused in our vocabulary. When you start thinking of pressure, it's because you've started to think of failure.*
>
> LOS ANGELES DODGERS MANAGER
> TOMMY LASORDA

I'm often asked how Arnold Palmer handles stress and pressure. My first inclination is to answer bluntly: "Not very well—because he works hard to manage the things that cause the stress in the first place."

Most successful professional athletes, especially Arnold Palmer, grow accustomed to the pressure of performance. They are shaped and forged in the crucible of competition. In his long and illustrious career, Arnie has ridden a roller coaster. There was the famous come-from-behind charge at Cherry Hills in 1960—and the infamous muffed putt on eighteen at the 1961 Masters. Having only to par the hole to win, Mr. Palmer scored a double-bogeyed six. The mistake cost him $8,000. In July of 1961, despite the wind and rain, the King pulled off a dramatic one-stroke victory at the British Open at Royal Birkdale. And then there was the crushing defeat in 1962 at the U.S. Open to Jack Nicklaus, followed two weeks later by a stunning performance at the British Open at Troon, where he successfully defended his title.

An ignorant or uninformed critic might suggest that Mr. Palmer was inconsistent, but the reality, of course, is quite the opposite. In February of 1970, the Associated Press named Arnie the "Athlete of the Decade"—a high honor, especially considering his competition: Bill Russell, Sandy Koufax, Johnny Unitas, Mickey Mantle, Willie Mays, and Jim Brown. The Associated Press saw Mr. Palmer for who he was—an amazing athlete who may not have always won, but a competitor who always showed, never gave up, and never gave in.

PRESSURE GROWS TALENT

The Brazilian game called *futebol de salão*[2] is similar to traditional World Cup soccer, but there are distinct differences. First, it's played indoors, and instead of playing eleven on eleven, it's five against five. The ball is smaller and heavier. Finally, the field is much smaller than your standard soccer field. In fact, *futebol de salão* translated means "soccer in the room" or "hall football." The result? Players are put under more pressure than in the soccer most of us are familiar with.

Daniel Coyle is the author of a great little book titled *The Talent Code: Greatness Isn't Born. It's Grown.*[3] Coyle examined the phenomenon of why so many great soccer players have come from Brazil. His conclusion? Brazilian kids are put under more pressure when learning to play the game because they learn by playing *futebol de salão*. The smaller teams mean each child touches the ball more, and the smaller field forces the smaller teams to more quickly develop critical ball-handling skills.

In short, pressure grows talent and improved talent produces better results.

JUST GO FOR IT!

I've also noticed that the more Arnold Palmer trusted me, the more I trusted myself. I had a greater degree of confidence and almost looked forward to high-pressure situations. Nothing beats jumping into the heat of the fire and learning how to survive.

Wayne Dyer is a world-renowned author and speaker who has dedicated his life to helping people realize their full potential. He's a strong advocate for taking on high-pressure challenges. "You'll seldom experience regret for anything that you've done," he has written. "It is what you haven't done that will torment you.

"The message, therefore, is clear. Do it!"[4]

Getting Into the Zone

LET's FACE IT. WHEN we're on the golf course, it's so easy to have our thoughts race between what has happened on past outings and what might occur going forward. These distracted or disjointed thoughts can take us on an emotional roller coaster and cause a loss of focus regarding what we want to accomplish.

Too many of us live a frantic and frenzied life. Our "margins" are narrow. We are reactionary in nature. We may dream, but we rarely plan and execute. We're constantly responding to other people's needs and demands. I have a friend who says he refuses to live off someone else's "out box," meaning just because it's a priority for them, it doesn't mean it has to be a priority for him. That may sound a little cynical, plus it's easier said than done.

Patience is also a form of action.
FRENCH SCULPTOR FRANÇOIS RODIN

BEWARE OF ESCALATING

As humans, we are prone to escalate rapidly in our emotions, connecting the feelings of one moment to the next, rather than isolating incidents. For example, if you're a father and you've just had a heated discussion with your teenage son, odds are your next conversation with your wife is unlikely to be the sweetest you've ever had. A wife who has had a rough day with toddlers is more likely to be short-tempered with her husband. Soon the whole house is upset and on edge. Have you ever noticed this pattern leading you from one problem to the next? It's like the guy who was trying to repair a slow drip under his sink. He grew so irritated at his inability to loosen the fitting that he took his wrench and smashed the PVC pipe to the main water line. Within two minutes, his entire kitchen was flooded. Bad move!

We often hear people gripe and groan. "I just can't catch a break!" they say. But are they paying attention to see their breaks, or are they so blinded by woe that they're looking in the opposite direction? If you look for trouble, trouble will always find you. It's simply the law of attraction.

The golf course is really no different. In fact, I've always thought the game of golf is a great metaphor for life. There's a natural tendency to react negatively when we hit a poor shot—when that's all it really is, just *one* poor shot! Our response often causes us to go into "fight or flight" mode without any awareness it's even happening. Granted, it's only natural to get caught up thinking about the outcome of our score, but impatience and irritation are always detrimental to the game, causing us to "force" shots.

BALANCING AGGRESSION WITH PATIENCE

I'm often asked who in the sport of golf today best exemplifies an approach similar to Arnold Palmer's "go for broke" style of play. Phil Mickelson, in my estimation, is the modern-day disciple of this approach. He's always taken charge on the course and been a highly focused player. There is intensity, but there's also something else: *patience*! Patience learned through failure! But, you might say, wouldn't a tendency toward aggressiveness contradict a penchant for patience? Not necessarily.

The key to finding your ideal "performance state" is by first calming down.

I often tell my students that the key to finding their ideal "performance state" is by first calming down so that they can eventually speed up. You'll note that I didn't say *slow* down; I said *calm* down. I borrow this insightful line of wisdom from life success mentor and coach Bob Proctor. He says, "You don't have to slow down, you must calm down. Because when you calm down, it will often allow you to speed up getting that which you want."

> *You don't have to slow down, you must calm down. Because when you calm down, it will often allow you to speed up getting that which you want.*[1]
>
> LIFE SUCCESS MENTOR BOB PROCTOR

For over fifty years, Arnold Palmer has followed the same routine before striking a shot in practice or in play. Prior to walking into his address position, he takes a massively deep breath through his nose, filling his entire chest cavity, and then calmly releases it through his mouth. If you're listening attentively, as I have done for thousands of his shots, the exhale sounds very much like a soft version of an old-time train engine releasing its steam. (Puff, puff, puff, puff, pufffffffffffff). I don't know if Arnie is even aware of this mannerism. The more important the shot, the more pronounced his breathing exercise becomes.

The next time you're watching a telecast of professional golf, take a moment to observe the behaviors outside of the actual swings. Study the players' body language and behavior. What do the majority of them do when they're preparing to hit that key shot? How do they look when they're walking around the cup preparing to make that winning putt? That's right, they usually appear calm and serene.

I liken the habits of Tiger Woods to those of a big cat circling its next meal. Tiger's walk is smooth and flowing. His eyes are wide open, bright and alert. If we had a heart monitor on him, I believe we would discover that his heartbeat is slowing through deep rhythmic breathing and quieting thoughts.

GETTING INTO THE ZONE

There is a difference between just waiting for something to happen and the habit of deliberately practicing patience. Patience is not waiting for something good to happen; that's just what I call wishful laziness. I like what professional golfer Johnny Miller said: "Serenity [in golf] is knowing that your worst shot is still pretty good." Again, Johnny's not suggesting it's okay to settle for second best; he's affirming the importance of self-confidence and the effectiveness of a calm and cool approach to the game.

> *Serenity [in golf] is knowing that your worst shot is still pretty good.*

GOLFER JOHNNY MILLER

It's possible to possess Palmer's aggressive approach to winning and remain calm in mind and approach. There's a lot of talk about athletes getting into "the zone." From my years of working with professional athletes, the typical star explains the zone like this: I am relaxed and tension free. Time seems to stop and decisions come quickly and easily. I see things fall into place moments before it actually happens. I am fearless and aggressive. I am calm and having fun creating what I want with no thought about how—I just do it.

Not surprisingly, research has confirmed these anecdotal reports. Roland A. Carlstedt, a clinical sports psychologist with Capella University in New York City, led a study designed to examine the internal thoughts of athletes during critical moments of competition. The findings?

Winning athletes possessed [a] hypnotic ability, but were not neurotic. They showed great skill in repressing negative thoughts and keeping their attention on the job at hand — a left-brain activity.

Those who crumbled also had the hypnotic ability, but their negative thoughts took over, especially at the most critical moments — a right-brain activity.

The ability to stop the transfer of intrusive thoughts — from the right brain to the left brain — is a crucial part of staying focused through crucial moments of competition.[2]

Taking time out of your life to calm down will actually help you speed up in getting what you really want. As silly as it might sound, I would encourage you to make the pursuit of quieting your mind a focal point of your life. How?

Meditation and prayer help us to calm our spirit and focus on the most important things. "Successful [people] will employ the latest and best-tested methods in production, distribution, and administration," Norman Vincent Peale wrote, "and many are discovering that one of the greatest of all efficiency methods is prayer power."[3] I couldn't agree more.

I'm currently using a fascinating software program called HeartMath,[4] initially designed by heart surgeons to help trauma victims develop control of their emotions through biofeedback and techniques in breathing and thinking. I have successfully used HeartMath in training golfers to understand the ideal performance state and how to shift into that state of coherence we call "the zone" through playing interactive video games with biofeedback. This incredible technology is helping many of my players reduce stress and develop a keen awareness of the mind and the body.

How golfers feel emotionally will greatly affect their actions and results. They might have perfect technique but think themselves into poor results. With practice, the disciplines learned through HeartMath allow golfers to control their emotions instead of the emotions controlling them.[5]

GETTING ON TRACK

After a state primary win leading up to the 1980 presidential election, George H. W. Bush famously declared that he had some "Big Mo" going. By "Big Mo," he was referring to momentum. The victory gave him and his team confidence, and though they eventually lost the nomination to Ronald Reagan, the Gipper thought enough of George Bush to place him on the ticket as vice president.

Momentum is a powerful force. It's an energy that's usually triggered by a series of small victories. If you're currently stuck in a rut or feel as though you're meandering without purpose or direction, here is the very best thing you can do: Look for an easy and simple success. If you're unhappy at work, prepare that résumé. If you want to reconnect with an old friend, write that letter. If you're estranged from a loved one, make the phone call. If you feel unorganized at home, clean out a closet. Looking for a new adventure? Sign up for that class. In other words, pick the low-hanging fruit. All too often, we allow a pursuit of perfection to become the enemy of good. Don't let what you can't do stop you from doing what you can do.

Write It Down

IF YOU HAVE EVER had an opportunity to play on a Palmer-designed golf course, there is a good chance that Erik Larsen held the topographical map as center lines were cut through the brush and thicket, and that it was he who felt the pitch of slope through his step as he walked every inch of all eighteen greens. Erik designs Arnold Palmer golf courses throughout the world, creating the masterpieces that we all are grateful for. He is a master at what he does, and I have always admired the creativity and attention to detail to create an amazing golf course—often over two hundred acres—a course that remains playable for all, environmentally sensitive, and natural in its completion.

Erik has a powerful little success secret he learned from Arnold Palmer—that of writing down your thoughts when they come to you and sorting them into action when most opportune. Sounds simple, doesn't it? So simple as to perhaps even be scoffed at. But this basic foundational practice has become an important action for many in harnessing and organizing the creative thoughts necessary for successful work.

COMMON SENSE
Erik Larsen

My great friend Bill Kubly is owner of Landscapes Unlimited and one of the finest golf course contractors in the world. We often play golf together, and during a recent outing, he excitedly informed me of a terrific gift idea he had come up with for friends and clients.

"Oh yes?" I was always on the lookout for a good idea. "What did you have in mind?"

Bill pulled from his pocket a cardholder that held 3x5-inch index cards. "This way people will have something for taking notes," he proudly informed me.

"But Bill," I said, reaching into my own pocket and pulling out a version of the cardholder that Arnold Palmer had given me twenty years earlier, "if you're going to give this for a gift, you should give the right kind!" Arnold's gift had a place for note cards—but it also included a spot for business cards and a small pencil.

Bill smiled and shrugged sheepishly. Leave it to Arnie to be ahead of his time.

My two-decades-old cardholder has been my constant companion. It's helped me to remember many important things and has provided me with a resource to collect and record my thoughts and ideas throughout the course of a day.

It's been said that common sense is sometimes the least common thing. Arnie wasn't the first person to impress upon me the importance of taking good notes and carrying around a tool to capture thoughts and ideas. Many, many years ago, my dad taught me to write things down in order to remember and follow through on what I promised to do. Dad realized that I had a habit of forgetting things—and absentminded people might be smart, but they're rarely successful. He used to tell me, "If it needs to be done, write it down!"

Technology has made note-taking a lot easier. We can email ourselves or text a friend or colleague nearly anywhere, anytime. iPhones even have dictation applications so that information can then be transcribed and emailed. Call me old-fashioned, but I still believe nothing trumps the tried-and-true method of pen and paper.

CAPTURING YOUR OWN GREAT IDEAS

Somebody once said that the art of communication is the language of leadership. If that's so, then learning to take good notes — clarifying and organizing ideas at the outset — is the beginning of Communication 101.

Do you remember playing the "telephone game" back when you were a kid? At the beginning, one person is fully briefed on a very specific message. That person is then instructed to relay the news to another person, but isn't allowed to write it down. Then the next person does the same thing. By the time the message is delivered, it's a garbled mess and usually a shell of its original form.

I've seen Arnie use index cards like cue cards to organize his thoughts and make sure that, when presenting to an audience, he could ensure personal callouts of gratitude for the participation and important roles of individuals. Sometimes I would even prepare the card for him with the key points and VIP list. He would never read a scripted speech; that is not his style. But rest assured, in his upper left-hand sport coat pocket would be a 3x5 card with the pertinent bulleted items that needed to be addressed. Interesting, though, how rarely we saw the card being pulled out. I guess it was just comforting to know that it was handy and that he was organized and ready to perform in his typical fearless and aggressive fashion.

Note-taking captures the power of ideas. Frankly, without ideas, we're nothing but blank slates. I believe God inspires people through various means and methods. If we listen, God will speak to us through our ideas, through our thoughts, and through inspiration. But we can only hold on to so much for so long. If we fail to capture and record an inspired thought around the time we first have it, we might very well never get it back again. Take captive the idea and gaff it with the lead end of a pencil!

> *Ideas are like slippery fish. When they come to you, you should gaff them with the lead of a pencil before they are lost.*
>
> MOTIVATIONAL SPEAKER AND AUTHOR
> EARL NIGHTINGALE

CAUGHT DOING SOMETHING RIGHT
Erik Larsen

When you're young and starry-eyed, you sometimes think that every minute with a celebrity or a genius must be scintillating and enlightening. I would learn pretty quickly that Arnie is all that—but he's also extremely practical.

Shortly after joining the Palmer team, I was invited to dine with Arnold and Winnie Palmer, as well as Winnie's mother and father, Mr. and Mrs. Walzer. Ed Seay, Arnie's golf course designer, also joined us at the Bay Hill Club & Lodge. I can remember being extremely quiet and quite content just to listen to the dinner banter. Soon the conversation turned to the importance of carrying around a pad to record notes, ideas, or assignments. Everyone, even Mr. and Mrs. Walzer, pulled out their cardholders.

Arnie turned toward me, expecting me, I think, to come up empty. But sure enough, I had the holder he had given me as a gift. I had passed another test! I was relieved to receive the knowing grin that made me feel like I was part of the Palmer team. More importantly, it showed him I had the tools with me to take care of business and get the job done.

Reading Erik's story about the cardholder sent me rummaging through my desk drawers, looking for ... ah, there it is, my own umbrella-embossed leather cardholder. He inspired me to dust if off and put this simple practice back to good use.

> *It's the little details that are vital. Little things make big things happen.*
>
> BASKETBALL COACH JOHN WOODEN

Those of us who work for Arnold Palmer like to frame our work with a simple motto: "The difference between ordinary and extraordinary is that little extra." And taking notes, capturing ideas, following up on assignments is often that little extra that makes a big difference.

> *The difference between ordinary and extraordinary is that little extra.*

Believe in a Dream

WHEN THE GOLF CHANNEL was launched on January 17, 1995, it was an unproven idea of Joseph E. Gibbs, an entrepreneur from Birmingham, Alabama. "There are 25 million [people] who live golf," Gibbs said then. "Too many have been treated as stepchildren when finalists come to the 18th hole and the networks say goodbye."[1]

At the time, a reporter for the *New York Times* admitted to having some misgivings about the viability of the network, but ultimately trusted the numbers. "There is a temptation to poke fun at the concept of the Golf Channel," Richard Sandomir wrote, "but it's not really nutty. Golf is a dependable TV product. Even if ratings aren't huge, viewers are wealthy and educated, the sort desired by the advertisers like the new venture's charter threesome: Titleist/Foot Joy, Nicklaus Golf Equipment and Izod."[2]

Arnold's belief in the dream, however, helped turn the Golf Channel from a mere concept to a cable network juggernaut. This I can say with certainty: without his commitment, the Golf Channel would not be where it is today.

"I went through a lot of discussions with Joe," said Palmer, "and I satisfied my curiosity, and the doubts that I had I also satisfied. I recognized Joe as a very brilliant person. And, of course, the negotiations and the things that went into starting the Golf Channel were very well thought out before we made it happen. There were questions like, What can you possibly show for twenty-four hours? So many things had to be worked out. But once we decided to do it, it was a done deal. It was now just getting it done!"

LOOKING BACK

The idea for the creation of the Golf Channel began to take shape at the 1990 PGA Championship, being held that year at Shoal Creek in Birmingham, Alabama. Interestingly, Joe Gibbs, a native of the area but not much of a golf fan at the time, had made his guest home available to one of the pros playing in the event. As fate would have it, that pro turned out to be Arnold Palmer, and the two men struck up a fast friendship.

"Those couple of days being with Arnold was all that was needed to change my mind about golf," Joe recalled. "I saw through Arnold the greatness in the game. And following him around, I'd never experienced the kind of enthusiasm that people had for him and the love they had for him. It overwhelmed me."

Twelve months after their initial introduction, Joe Gibbs presented to Arnold Palmer his vision and plans for a 24/7 cable channel solely dedicated to golf. Mr. Palmer's initial reaction was one of intrigue, but he was noncommittal and even a little hesitant. It would, after all, be the first of its kind on television.

"I had some reservations, but I liked the idea very much," Arnie recalled. "Twenty-four hours is a lot of golf. I had to think about that. But the more I thought about it—the more I deeply thought about it—I began to think it would work because there are so many aspects of it you can use."

Arnold eventually became Joe's 50 percent partner and cofounder, with each investing the seed money for the initial $6 million expenditure. Joe became the company's CEO, and

Arnold assumed the role of chairman of the board. Though it wouldn't hit the air until 1995, the Golf Channel was officially formed in July of 1992.

SLOW GROWTH

The fortunes of the channel didn't always look so promising, however. Gibbs once told me that back in December 1993, over a year before the network eventually launched, he was at a breaking point.

"We'd spent all of our original investment," he said. "About $6 million. The options on all our contracts were up. I'd been out there on the street for six months trying to raise the money we needed to make it a go, and things weren't looking very promising."

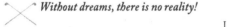 *Without dreams, there is no reality!*

LUIS B. COUTO

Joe Gibbs went to Arnold and laid out the reality of the situation. "Here's where we are," he said. "Our options are we can shut this whole thing down, walk away, and write off our investment, or we can go back out, get in deeper, and give it one more shot."

How did Arnie respond? "He just looked at me straight," Joe recalled, "and said, 'I don't want to quit.'"

People have asked me about Mr. Palmer's commitment to the Golf Channel and why he was so determined to make it work. After all, he had plenty of money and power and prestige, the normal things that drive so many competitive people. Was it something else?

The answer is quite simple, really. You see, the very thing that motivated Mr. Palmer to make the Golf Channel a success is what kept him going all throughout his career. Arnold Palmer has a "drive" that can be summed up in the acronym DRIVE:

Determination: For Arnie, if it's worth doing, it's worth doing well.

Responsibility: As the King of golf, Arnold Palmer feels a certain obligation to give back to the people and to the sport that has given him so much.

Inspiration: Arnie sees himself as an ambassador of the game. He enjoys helping others reach their full potential—whether it's a weekend golfer looking to improve his game or a sponsor who is willing to stand behind the Palmer brand.

Vision: Mr. Palmer has a gift for seeing what could be—the mark of a true visionary.

Energy: Since the Lord has blessed Arnie with good health and vitality, the King of golf enjoys making the very most of every minute of every day.

The Golf Channel was launched in a modest office park less than ten miles from Arnold Palmer's Bay Hill Club in southwest Orlando. When the channel first started operations, it had approximately one hundred employees. Even by the end of the first year on air, it looked like the channel was going to be a huge success—the subscriber count reached twice its year-end projection at 1.4 million, and the advertising revenues were well above all expectations. By the end of 1996, the channel had launched its own website, televised the first of many Senior PGA Tour events, partnered with FOX Broadcasting Company on a $50 million equity contribution arrangement, and, along with a partner, established the network in Japan. By then, seven million people were subscribing, a figure that was to double by the end of 1997.

ONWARD AND UPWARD

Less than ten years from their first meeting, Joe Gibbs and Arnold Palmer had taken an idea, made a commitment, and turned it into one of golf's and television's greatest success stories. With the company's valuation estimated at $678 million, the two partners sold their controlling interests in 2001 to the cable giant Comcast. Today, the Golf Channel is available in seventy million households and delivers programming that now reaches 90 percent of the world's golfers.

The Golf Channel story is a living and breathing testament to many of the traits illustrated in this book. But above all else, the story of its genesis illustrates the power of chasing a dream — and the payoff that comes when you refuse to give up.

Practice Like a Pro

IT WAS A LATE Orlando evening in April, and we were tucked away on the back of the range, a spot reserved for Academy lessons and PGA Tour professionals who were also Bay Hill members. It had every feel of Florida about it, but from the conversation taking place, you would have imagined we were four hundred miles north in Augusta, Georgia. Arnold Palmer quite clearly had Georgia on his mind.

As the evening unfolded, he began narrating with specific detail each of his desired shots for the upcoming four-day tournament. Officials at Augusta rotate the "pin positions" (hole placements) on a daily basis. Arnie being Arnie, he had memorized all seventy-two of them and was now mentally and physically executing the perfectly struck golf shots desired for each one as part of his preparation.

> *There's nothing remarkable about it. All one has to do is hit the right keys at the right time and the instrument plays itself.*
> COMPOSER JOHANN SEBASTIAN BACH

This is a grand example of what successful people do to consistently achieve greatness. They don't just show up, set up, and try for the best. The steps in the march toward victory begin weeks — if not months or years — in advance.

PRACTICE, PRACTICE, PRACTICE

A friend once told me of a trip he took to New York City. After an overnight flight, he checked into his hotel room and planned to get some rest before an evening presentation. His sleep was fitful, thanks to the annoying strains of disjointed violin music coming from the room next door. It went on for hours. Frankly, it didn't sound like much of anything, but having a daughter who was taking lessons, he had a soft heart and endured it.

By mid-afternoon, he was hungry and decided to leave his room for a bite to eat. Just as he left his room, the door next to his opened, and a woman in a long black dress exited. She was carrying a hard black case. Trying to be polite, my friend said, "Are you a musician?"

"Yes," she said quietly.

"You look like you're going to a performance," he replied.

"I am. I'm guest performing with the New York Philharmonic."

The woman was a professional musician! Her profession might appear quite glamorous when she's onstage, but she was an elite performer because she was willing to persist and carry out very unglamorous work behind the scenes.

QUESTIONS AND ANSWERS

Years later, back inside his Latrobe office, I decided to ask Arnie about his infamous practice routine. I described a particular practice session. "I have to say that one of my most memorable occasions with you was the week before Augusta, observing you prepare for the Masters Tournament. I recall us being on the Academy end of the practice range at Bay Hill, and your intensity and enthusiasm were so different than any other practice I had observed.

"The best was when you said to me, 'What shot would you like to see me play?' I thought to myself, *How cool is this that I'm going to get to play Augusta National through Arnold Palmer's thoughts, feelings, and actions.* I said to you, 'Okay, let me see your tee shot off the first hole during the final round.' Immediately I saw you transformed with a youthful and confident enthusiasm. To hear you illustrate the nuances of the shot you were about to execute, it was almost like you were there at Augusta on the first hole on that final day. How real was that visualization practice for you?"

A serious look came across his face. "It was very real," he replied. "I could imagine myself being there as close as my memory could recall with full color, feels, and even the smells, for that matter. My fond memories of Augusta National and especially the Masters week are so revered and emotionally powerful to me. I can remember the details of things that happened forty years ago as crystal clear, as if it all just occurred."

I've been around hundreds of excellent competitive golfers and played professionally myself for many years. Yet I had never seen such loving intensity and focus with each practice ball struck. Each one struck had its importance tattooed firmly with a spirit of the King's persistence and determination.

"When did you begin to practice like this during your playing career, and how often would you practice like this before a tournament?" I asked. "Was this unique for Augusta, or did you have this similar intensity for every event?"

"Well, let me think a moment," he said. "I learned to plan my work from Byron Nelson. He wrote about it in his book, and as a boy I read about it and began to apply the practice of playing the course in my mind before every important round. As I became more seasoned and had played the circuit for a few years, the ability to remember certain nuances of the greens and hole layouts and certain pin placements that the Tournament would seem to select for certain days of the event became very predictable. Especially Augusta. I know where the Thursday through Sunday pins will be, and so do the other guys that have played in the event. So when I see these shots in my mind, I am confident that these are the correct shots to execute for each round of the event."

I wondered whether it was important to remember or ponder his missed shots. "We know you have a library of great shots and moments. What about the poor shots and failures? Do you keep inventory of these as well?"

"Oh, I suppose," he admitted, "but certainly I don't dwell on them. Whenever I didn't execute on the shot that I wanted, this would usually fire me up to work on that certain shot so that I knew, when I faced a similar shot again, I was ready to execute correctly and with confidence the next time around. I will also add that I never spent much time worrying or being concerned about the shots I missed. Rather I got my head wrapped around doing it right and put it to task again as soon as I could, with nothing but great expectations."

THE POWER OF IMAGINATION

Arnold Palmer's simulated Masters practice sessions introduced the importance of using memory and imagination to practice with a purpose. Many of us tend to just hit balls and think mostly about the technique of our swing. We think just hitting the ball longer and straighter will solve our problems. But the best players get better because they are creating shots that begin in the *mind*. They condition mental faculties that increase their confidence and improve their ability to execute certain shots during practice and transfer that talent out onto the course.

Arnold Palmer has emphasized the importance of never being too concerned over the missed shots, but working diligently in practice to build confidence that he could repeat a certain shot the next time he faced a similar challenge. I would encourage you to try this "practice like a pro" approach toward the end of your next practice session.

This approach has widespread applicability as much off the golf course as it does on it. What's your dream? What's your goal?

Let's start small. Suppose your goal is to have a more harmonious home. Did you know that experts have found that the first five minutes of anything—especially the first five minutes coming home to your kids—will most often set the tone and determine the mood for the rest of the event? Have you ever thought about "practicing" in your mind how you'd like that time to go? I'm not suggesting that life should be scripted, but a little plotting and planning goes a long way. I know a man who likes to call home at the end of the day when he's about thirty minutes away. By doing so, he's attempting to take the temperature of the family and prepare himself mentally for what he'll find upon his arrival. He then has time to prepare an encouraging word or comment for his kids, as opposed to being ambushed with the latest drama of the day when he walks in the door.

Maybe you're dreaming about starting a new business. Dreams are good, but dig a little deeper. If you want to open your own travel business, it might be a good idea to visit with someone who is already doing it. Ask about their typical day, week, or month. How does it fit into your lifestyle?

Don't just show up and expect good things to happen. Former NBA Hall of Famer Larry Bird once said that when he was young, he refused to leave the court until he had perfected whatever he was working on that day. "My dream," he said, "was to become a pro."

As we all know, he *became* a pro because he *practiced* like a pro.

Capitalize on Your Success

AT ONE TIME, CZECHOSLOVAKIAN-BORN Ivan Lendl, now an American citizen, was the number one tennis player in the world. His statistics are legendary: eight career Grand Slam titles and more than a thousand wins.[1] Now fifty years old, Ivan is retired and thoroughly enjoying the game of golf. Not surprisingly, he attacks his new hobby with a zest and zeal similar to the passion with which he played professional tennis.

I am thankful to be friends with Ivan and invited him to offer some perspective for you on the practice and preparation of a champion:

PLAY TO YOUR STRENGTHS
Ivan Lendl

Champions draw energy from anything and everything—the hype of a big match, a negative comment, a spontaneous challenge, or a certain German player you really want to beat. You think to yourself, *I've got to play hard and show them!* Successful players are always up for a good challenge and almost always rise to the occasion.

Champions draw energy from success; it's what separates them from the others. Some good players are motivated by a poor performance, a disappointment, or an embarrassing outing. They may wind up working harder to not let it happen again, but the majority of these athletes will get complacent and grow content with a certain level of success. They don't continue to work as hard to improve; "good" is good enough. This is the big difference between good players and great players. The great ones are inspired by success, whereas average players are moved (and irritated) more by a poor showing.

> *You were born to win, but to be a winner, you must plan to win, prepare to win, and expect to win.*
> MOTIVATIONAL SPEAKER AND AUTHOR
> ZIG ZIGLAR

People have asked me: From where does the difference come? I believe you learn it, as I did, by observing the great players and from just being around them. As a boy, I spent many hours at a tennis club. I would just watch them do certain things certain ways and begin mimicking their good habits. It's been my observation that you can take any kid and have them hang out with a great performer and they will invariably and naturally pick up on the work ethic and begin thinking like the players they're hanging around with. The more time a child spends with a great player, the better his or her chances of becoming a great player will be.

I have matured and mellowed with age, but I still hate to lose. In fact, I hate to lose at anything that I do! Having spent time in clubhouses and locker rooms, I've discovered this is a common thread woven through the psyche of all competitive athletes. Some might say, "I love to win," or, like Palmer has said, "I was afraid of losing, and that fear inspired me." However you slice or dice the words, the sentiment is the same.

My coach used to regularly tell me, "Ivan, the more sweat on the practice field, the less blood on the battlefield." He was right! I loved to thoroughly and diligently prepare for my matches. When the time came for the match, I always believed that I was more ready than anyone. This habit gave me a mental edge. All the great players enjoy their time of preparation. In fact, they seem to have almost unlimited energy when doing so. Once the time for competition arrives, the great athlete will let the instincts take over and simply focus on the pursuit of victory.

I've discovered that positive mental imaging is quite different in golf than it is in tennis. Since you're competing against yourself in golf and someone else in tennis, your strategy for success is naturally going to be different. For example, in golf, you always want to play to your strengths and stay away from your weaknesses. Like Gary Player's strength is hitting a low draw and Tiger Woods's is the high fade. These are the shots they are most comfortable playing and should be what they go to when needed to execute under pressure. You're not afforded the same luxury when it comes to playing tennis. Most opponents are quick to identify your patterns and they do what they can to play away from your strengths and capitalize on your weaknesses. Of course, you're doing the exact same thing to them.

My preparation for big matches was to watch film with colored pencils and chart certain serves at different pressure situations in the match. Even though these great players were pretty good at masking their moves, statistics and outcomes don't lie. I would always thoroughly study my opponent's tendencies in very specific shots and situations and, when given the opportunity, capitalize on their weakness and attempt to play to my strength.

I cannot compete at tennis anymore, but I still love to compete while playing golf. It's funny how perspectives change; I used to think golf was an old man's sport, but now that I'm fifty, my peers seem pretty young and spry! I still love to prepare, even if it is for a mini-tour event of a Pro-Am. I will give all I have to be ready to win. It's hard to teach an old dog new tricks. But it's not impossible.

In Pat Williams's book *How to Be Like Mike,*[2] Pat writes how Michael Jordan would often pick fights with his fellow teammates during practice sessions if he felt the intensity level needed to be raised. Why? Michael believed that practice was more important than the game and that the energy exhausted throughout the preparatory process gave him and his teammates the greatest chance to excel and perform during the most critical points in the game.

To put it simply, if I don't practice the way I should, then I won't play the way that I know I can.

It's always been fascinating for me to work with professional athletes, but it's especially fun to assist an individual who has achieved world-class status in a completely different sport. Getting to know Ivan Lendl, I've been reminded that raw talent is important, but talent alone won't turn something good into something great. Nurturing, shaping, and perfecting athletic talent is as much an art as it is a skill. But nothing beats the habit and discipline of persistent practice.

I've always been struck by supervisors who seem to spend an inordinate amount of time trying to point out all of the faults and weaknesses of their staff. A little tough love with constructive criticism is a good thing, but you can very easily crush a person's spirit by focusing too intently on areas that need improvement.

Instead, "catch" them doing something right and try to build on their strengths.

When it comes to the habits of preparation, Arnold Palmer is no different than Ivan Lendl or Michael Jordan. All three men regularly emphasize working hard and working smart, channeling their energy into the best practice sessions not just to compete well—but to perform well enough to win.

PART 5

A True Champion's Attitude Is Gratitude

From the beginning, it was drilled into me that a golf course was a place where character fully reveals itself—both its strengths and its flaws. As a result, I learned early not only to fix my ball marks but also to congratulate an opponent on a good shot, avoid walking ahead of a player preparing to shoot, remain perfectly still when someone else was playing, and a score of other small courtesies that revealed, in my father's mind, one's abiding respect for the game.

ARNOLD PALMER

The Gratitude Attitude

Successful people think and do things in a certain way, and enjoying the journey begins and ends with their attitude. What is attitude? Motivational guru Bob Proctor suggests that attitude is quite simply a compilation of your thoughts, feelings, and actions. I think he's right.

> *Attitude is quite simply a compilation of your thoughts, feelings, and actions.*
> MOTIVATIONAL GURU BOB PROCTOR

Many people assume they have a good attitude because, on the surface, they refrain from thinking negatively or embracing a defeatist mentality. But a person's attitude is best measured by how their thoughts morph into feelings, which then translate into action and produce results. Proctor has said, "Gratitude keeps you connected to your source of supply, that being the infinite power of God."

Science is finally beginning to reckon with the physical, emotional, and spiritual power of a grateful person. In study after study, people who are thankful for things—big or small—report being happier, less stressed, and healthier than people who are not. Roman philosopher and statesman Cicero once said, "Gratitude is not only the greatest of the virtues but the parent of all the others."

Gratitude lies at the very center and heart of Christianity. After all, Jesus Christ died for the sake of our sins—he paid the price for our transgressions—and gave us the promise of eternal life.

I have journeyed alongside Arnold Palmer for the past quarter century and have seen him exhibit this attitude of gratitude time and time again. He is a grateful man who gives the credit for a good life to his great and glorious Maker. Because Mr. Palmer is a gentleman from an older generation, he's a man who considers his faith to be a sacred and somewhat private affair. He is not comfortable in the pulpit and instead prefers to let his life speak his faith. There is a quiet strength behind that habit. It's powerful.

Yes, Arnold Palmer is a man clearly infused with an attitude of gratitude.

Don't Dwell on Yesterday's News

A TOURNAMENT WIN IS a benchmark in a Tour professional's career. It's also likely to be a greatly cherished memory, and I've come to notice how many champions memorialize their great feats by designating a room in their home for the trophies and memories. Some outsiders looking in would consider them to be shrines to their great achievements.

I've also noticed how many athletes, after reaching the pinnacle, don't seem to produce the same results after their big victory. In fact, after big wins, there have been many times when very successful golfers slid into a slump and sometimes even disappeared from the leader board, never to be seen again.

How does this happen? What is the difference between the one-hit wonder and the few great ones who keep winning? And why don't some continue in their winning ways?

I was about to find out.

No Room in the Inn

A short time after having been hired as the director of Arnold Palmer's Golf Academy, I was invited to the Palmers' home for dinner. I arrived a few minutes early that evening, and Mrs. Palmer greeted me at the door.

"Arnie is still getting ready, Brad," she told me. "He will be down shortly."

Knowing that she was busy preparing dinner and not wanting

to be a bother, I asked if it would be all right for me to take a self-guided tour of the "trophy room." With Arnold Palmer's ninety-two lifetime Tour wins, I thought his trophy room must be a sight to see.

"Oh, I'm sorry, Brad," she replied, "we don't have such a room."

I was puzzled but dropped the subject. Later that evening, however, during dinner conversation, my curiosity got the best of me. "Mr. Palmer," I began, "ninety-two Tour wins — that's a lot of hardware! So how come you have no trophy display?"

Arnie put down his fork, looked me straight in the eye, and said, quite excitedly, "For what? That's yesterday's news!" After a brief pause and that characteristic confident grin of his, he went on to explain.

Nostalgia is a seductive liar.
AMERICAN DIPLOMAT GEORGE W. BALL

"Don't take me wrong, Brad, I have enjoyed every victory and greatly cherish the memories. We've even celebrated a little bit after each one. But come Monday morning of the next week, I'm no different than the man who missed the cut last week. In fact, he is probably hungrier than I am. So if I am to be competitively ready, I must get my thoughts off yesterday and deal with today. There will be a day when I can take the time to look back. But as long as I want to stay competitive, I must never stop and marvel at what I have accomplished — only forward to my next challenge at hand."

As long as I want to stay competitive, I must never stop and marvel at what I have accomplished — only forward to my next challenge at hand.

ARNOLD PALMER

ETERNAL PERSPECTIVE

James Dobson is a child psychologist, author, and radio talk show host. Although he's never played professional golf, he once considered himself a rising and budding tennis prospect. At eighteen years of age, Jim Dobson arrived on the campus of Pasadena College with a singular goal. Here is the story in his own words:

> I loved tennis. I come from south Texas, and I played tennis down there eleven months out of the year, six days a week, two or three hours a day, and all day Saturday. I really loved to play tennis. I never would have been great, but I was developing some ability in tennis.
>
> I arrived on campus before the other students got there, went over to the Administration Building—kind of strolling around, getting the feel of the campus. I remember walking up to this trophy case. There were the trophies from past athletic victories that the college had had—mostly basketball. In the center of this case was a tennis trophy, about two-foot high. They build them five-foot high today, but in those days, that was a big trophy. It was spiral. It had a cylinder in the center of it, and on it were the names of the students who won the school tournament every year back to 1947. Here were the tennis greats at Pasadena College where I was a student.
>
> I remember salivating as I stood before that trophy case. I looked at that list of names, and I said, "Someday, someday, my name is going to be engraved on the tennis trophy. I'm going to get my name on there as the best tennis player in this school." I had that as a goal. It's hard to believe today that that would be that important to me. It's interesting how your values change over time.

But as an eighteen-year-old, that was one of the chief goals of my life — to win the school tournament and to get my name, especially, on that trophy, so that freshmen, ten years later, would come and stand before that case and look at my name among the tennis greats. That tells you a little bit about my ego needs at that time. As it turned out, I succeeded in 1957 and 1958. I won the school tournament, and they duly engraved my name on the trophy. That was my legacy to future generations.

I left the school many years ago. About ten years ago, the son of my friend Will Spaite was on the campus of Pasadena College rummaging around, looking for something, and he found that trophy in the trash. My trophy, with my name on it, and all the tennis greats down through the years since 1947. It had been thrown away. He rescued it, took it home, and they cleaned it up, and Will brought me that trophy. So I have it in my office today, and there my name is. I might say, the school didn't even record my 1958 victory, so I'm going to engrave it on there myself.

Isn't that an illustration of the way life works? If you live long enough, life will trash your trophies. There are only two things that matter: serving God and being acceptable to him and hearing these words, "Well done, thou good and faithful servant," and being ushered into the kingdom forever and ever. The second thing is to take as many as possible with you on that journey into eternity, to serve them while you're here on earth, and to embrace them, and share your faith, and eventually take them with you to meet the Savior on the other side — beginning with your own flesh and blood. That's where the value system ought to start; that's where the priorities begin. When it's all said and done, there isn't anything else. When you look at it in eternal values that will last—that will stand the test of time—there's nothing else even in that league. If we feel that way, then we ought to be living our lives accordingly.[1]

There are better things ahead than any we leave behind.

OXFORD PROFESSOR AND AUTHOR

C. S. LEWIS

What is the trophy in your life? Might it be the graduate degree you're thinking about pursuing—a noble endeavor, but one that might mean several years' worth of time away from your kids and spouse? Is it the pursuit of the corner office and the big promotion? Is it the new car? The bigger house?

Taking the long view of life is a challenging habit to acquire, but it's well worth the energy and effort.

Befriend Your Enemies

THE PROFESSIONAL RIVALRY BETWEEN Arnold Palmer and Jack Nicklaus is legendary, but the personal friendship between these two giants of the game is among the most enduring in all of sports. Some have referred to their relationship as a "complicated friendship" and others as a study between a bull and a bear.

An interesting narrative of the Palmer/Nicklaus rivalry has emerged over the years. Because controversy sells and noise makes news, popular media have tried to paint a picture of a highly spirited and contentious relationship. It's true they've had their moments. "We've had moments when we've disagreed," Nicklaus said, "we've had moments when we fought each other right down to the end of the tournament, and we've had moments when we've fought each other for last place."[1]

Arnold agreed. "There have been times when we've fought each other so hard that we've let others go by us. But frankly, I think our rivalry, if that's what you want to call it, would have been even more intense if we were the same age."[2]

So the truth, as often is the case with stories that unfold over time, lies somewhere in the middle. While it's true there has been tension between the two men over the years, the totality of the relationship has easily been a net positive.

In the following story, Jack shares his thoughts on a pivotal time in his rookie year on the Tour. It came when Arnie and Jack were locked in the heat of battle, but, even more importantly, it came at a critical point in Nicklaus's young career. Contrary to the picture of confrontation that the media enjoy painting in our minds between the two, Jack will explain how the bonds of friendship were forged and solidified.

THE GENTLEMAN
Jack Nicklaus

When Arnold Palmer and I stepped onto the eighteenth tee in the final round of the 1962 Phoenix Open, I was tied for second with Billy Casper. Arnold had a twelve-stroke lead, so the only competition that day was to see who the runner-up would be. I needed a birdie to finish second in the tournament. This was the first time he and I had been paired together competitively, and as Arnold reached for his driver, he stopped for a moment and looked directly at me, a sandy-haired, twenty-two-year-old rookie. I will never forget what he said.

"Relax," Arnold whispered with a smile and a wink. "You can birdie this hole. You can finish second in this tournament and that would be a great thing for you."

I did birdie that hole and took home a whopping $3,400 check. But the bigger thing I took home that day was a great deal of admiration and respect for a champion who had spoken such kind words to me. That was Arnold Palmer.

Arnold and I played many times together after that day in Phoenix, whether it was as competitors in tournaments or Big Three events or as partners in international team competitions. We played against each other in his backyard (Oakmont in the 1962 U.S. Open) and together in my backyard (one example was winning the 1966 PGA National Team Championship together in Palm Beach Gardens, Florida), and we played all over the world. Our wives were good friends, and he was always a good companion and a good playing partner. We spent a lot of time together.

Much has been made of the rivalry between Arnold and me. Sure, our play has always been wonderfully competitive, but never bitter. I often had to fight (figuratively speaking) Arnold's gallery—the infamous "Arnie's Army"—but I never had to fight the man. It was and still is a friendly rivalry. I consider Arnold one of my closest friends in the game.

I destroy my enemy when I make him my friend.
ABRAHAM LINCOLN

That doesn't mean that every time we went out there, we didn't want to beat each other's brains in. As vigorous competitors, we never were satisfied with losing to each other and always looked forward to competing against each other. For over forty-five years we have gone toe-to-toe, shot-for-shot. Too often we found ourselves playing each other more than the golf course. And though I hate to admit it, this cost us more than one tournament.

When we see each other, we still love to share a laugh and a needling of the other. I remember in the spring of 2006, Arnold and I were filming a CBS special sponsored by the Royal Bank of Scotland. We were talking about the 1960 U.S. Open at Cherry Hills when Arnold rallied to victory. That was the Open when I played with Ben Hogan and actually led well into the final nine holes. But Arnold shot thirty to leapfrog me and a few others.

"If I hadn't shot thirty-nine the last nine holes, no one would have ever heard of Arnold Palmer," I quipped.

Arnold quickly volleyed back, "Yeah, sort of like if I

hadn't missed three chips at Oakmont, no one would have heard of Nicklaus."

Golf fans today take the game's popularity for granted. But Arnold Palmer is the reason. He brought along a whole new fan base and made golf attractive to the television-viewing public. He had a look and an aggressive style of play that endeared him to avid and casual fans alike. Arnold also had — and still has — an insatiable appetite for the game of golf. Whether it's playing in a Skins Game or just out for a round with friends at Bay Hill, Arnold loves to play the game. People from all walks of life recognize and appreciate that.

In golf, there never has been anyone like Arnold Palmer and there probably won't be another like him again. He was more popular than anybody. It didn't matter then who you were and it doesn't matter now. Arnold was always the competitor ... but always the gentleman and friend.

Because professional golf is predominantly an individual sport where success and failure usually rest on one person, egotists are a dime a dozen on the Tour. But then there are stories like this one, where one star helps to shape and nurture another.

I have read many accounts of the closeness between the two men, but none more powerful than Jack's recollection of how the two reached out to each other in 1999 after the death of Arnie's beloved wife, Winnie.

When Winnie died of cancer in 1999, the Nicklaus family was watching their thirty-year-old son, Gary, attempt to earn his PGA Tour card after eight failed attempts. Palmer tried to convince Jack that he should stay with his son, but Jack and Barbara came to the funeral. After the service, Jack was getting updates on his cell phone. Arnold asked how Gary was doing.

"He's got a couple of holes to play," Jack said.

"Well, come on, let's turn on TV," Arnie said.

"You don't have to do that," Jack said.

"I would want to," Arnold said.

Gary shot sixty-three in his sixth and final round and earned his Tour card.

Overcome by joy and sadness, the two old rivals fell into each other's arms and cried.

The long and layered relationship between Arnold Palmer and Jack Nicklaus is a good reminder that just because you're "enemies" on the course doesn't mean you can't be friends for life off the course.

Respect for Every Man

I WAS A ROOKIE with the Arnold Palmer Golf Management Company, working at the Turtle Bay Hilton on the North Shore of Oahu, when I had my first real encounter with Arnold Palmer. On that day, an entourage came driving into the resort with two stretch limos and several town cars following behind. It was like the buzz surrounding a rock star or, better yet, a royal entourage! Trailing behind this train was the golf course superintendent's rusted-out Chevy truck. I watched it turn away from the caravan and head toward the maintenance shed, and I didn't give it much thought.

I went about my business, but twenty minutes later I received a call in the pro shop from the hotel manager asking that I please find Mr. Palmer. The local dignitaries had arrived and were waiting to meet with him at a reception in the main hotel. I told the manager that Mr. Palmer could be anywhere on the property. Well, I was told, Arnie had ridden in from the airport with Mike Homna, our golf course superintendent. If I found Mike, I would find Mr. Palmer. So Arnie had been riding with Mike in that beat-up old Chevy truck!

Armed with my new intel, I headed down to the maintenance facility. As I turned into the employee lunch room, there was Mr. Palmer, sitting on a wooden picnic bench with the entire grounds staff, sharing a sandwich right out of a lunch pail.

"Excuse me, Mr. Palmer," I said, a bit nervous to interrupt mid-sentence. "The governor and other dignitaries are awaiting your arrival at the hotel."

Arnie turned, smiled, and calmly replied to me, "Please tell them that I will be there shortly." Then he returned to his conversation with the crew.

The King, knowing his schedule that day, understood that his only window of opportunity to show his appreciation and gratitude to his team of workers was to steal a moment away and just make it happen.

Arnold Palmer's thankful attitude has grown into an oak tree of gratitude shared with many people—especially his army of fans, Arnie's Army. Throughout my employment, I have observed in Palmer a consistent penchant for expressing appreciation and respect for others. Including a punk kid dressed in surf clothes who became one of golf's great success stories.

PAYING ATTENTION TO A PUNK KID

For those who follow the sport of golf, Jason Gore's story is a familiar one. As a youngster, he dreamed of playing professional golf and making it to the big tournaments. He worked hard, sacrificed mightily, and eventually his dream came true. But when he was eleven years old, something big happened to little Jason, something that truly changed the course of his life. While visiting some friends in Pittsburgh, he convinced his mother to drive him to the Latrobe Country Club. He had no invitation, of course, but he was too naïve to let that stop him.

"I was wearing a light blue Town & Country surf design T-shirt with a big, ugly emblem on the back," he remembered, "along with a pair of horribly obnoxious multi-colored shorts. I had never been on a surfboard in my life, but I looked like a surfer."[1]

As fate would have it, the Gores asked for Arnold, who just happened to be at the club that day. Jason and Mr. Palmer met. They had a pleasant exchange and even took a few photographs. But then something even more special happened.

"He said, 'Son, I'm going to go hit balls. Would you like to come watch?' I sat right on the little slope behind the first tee and watched Mr. Palmer hit balls for about forty-five minutes. And from that point on, I knew I wanted to be a professional golfer."[2]

> *A fellow who does things that count, doesn't usually stop to count them.*
>
> ALBERT EINSTEIN

We never stand so tall, someone once said, as when we stoop to help a child. Jason Gore, who has now been playing on the Tour since 1997,[3] would surely concur.

"The littlest things he does for a punk dressed in surf clothes who was trespassing on his property changes lives," Gore said. "He's got that power, and that's what makes him the King. That's why he's the greatest person to this game."[4]

AN ATTITUDE OF GRATITUDE

I have admired Mr. Palmer's "gratitude attitude" since the first day we met. Every year, I'm honored to be a part of the "Champions for Children" charity fundraiser for the Arnold Palmer Hospital for Children. I've had a chance to speak with John Bozard, the CEO of Arnold Palmer Hospitals, about Arnie's personal involvement. He's told me some pretty incredible stories about all that the Palmer family has done quietly and without publicity. Back when the idea of a hospital dedicated entirely to the needs of children was only a dream, John took Arnie on a tour of the facilities available at the time. "It just seems like we can do better than this for our kids," Palmer said as they walked the halls. When it came time to decide whether Mr. Palmer would help, he jumped into the project feet first.

"That man has kept his word on every commitment," John said. "He's far exceeded our expectations, not only in his personal giving—his personal giving is well into the millions of dollars—but just our association with the tournament and with him and the other folks that he has brought in, we can recognize well over $50 million associated with the Palmer connection. So it has been a wonderful thing for our organization."

Mr. Palmer's longtime aide and right-hand man, Donald "Doc" Giffen, has had the opportunity to know both father and son. "I had just lost Finnegan, my best friend, in a plane crash," Doc recalled, "and Arnie's dad and I were headed out together on a trip. He turned to me—we were sitting on the plane—and said, 'I know you lost one of your best buddies; I'll try and be your friend.'"

Arnie later told me, "[That type of kindness] rubbed off on me. I think my father was that way in everything he did. He was just a good guy."

If there is a common theme found within these pages, it would be that when people point to Arnold Palmer's good habits and generous spirit, Arnie quickly points toward someone else—namely his parents—and suggests they deserve the credit.

"My father was a very gracious guy," Mr. Palmer has told me. "He was the toughest guy I ever knew, but he was also the most gracious and the kindest. Oh, was he kind. He did things for people his entire life and never once expected anything in return."

With deep and strong roots established long ago by his father, in Arnold Palmer's economy, no man is more important than the next and every stranger is really just a friend he hasn't yet met.

Always Grateful

BEING ONE OF THE most revered celebrity athletes of all time comes at a steep price, and few people realize just how much of Palmer's time is spent simply signing his name. When Arnold is in his office at Bay Hill and mired in meetings, it's not unusual for him to be signing autographs the entire time. Fans usually mail him a postage-paid envelope in which to return the item, but if they don't, Arnie pays the bill. As a result, Arnold Palmer Enterprises incurs thousands upon thousands of dollars for postage each year—but they do so happily and without complaint. All told, by conservative estimates, Mr. Palmer signs approximately 100,000 items annually for fans and charity fundraisers.

I was recently called into a meeting in Arnie's office to discuss a new golf academy location in Dallas, and throughout our discussion he never stopped signing golf balls, hats, clubs, artwork, photos, Pennzoil cans, baby shoes, and more. One secretary would unbox and feed him an item for his signature, and another would take the signed item out of his left hand and repack it for shipping. After watching this for about an hour, I asked, "Don't you ever get tired of this?"

> *I would maintain that thanks are the highest form of thought;*
> *and that gratitude is happiness doubled by wonder.*
> ENGLISH WRITER AND CHRISTIAN APOLOGIST
> G. K. CHESTERTON

"As long as they ask," he replied, "I am flattered. In fact, it would be a sad day if they stopped."

My wife, business partner, and dearest friend, Wanda—who has seen Arnie both up front and behind the scenes and has heard all the war stories of our friends who have served him—has experienced firsthand Mr. Palmer's grateful (and gracious) attitude toward his fans, as she shares in this story.

MY PERSONAL WITNESS OF THE
KING'S ATTITUDE OF GRATITUDE
Wanda Brewer

In 1986, Brad was honored to help Mr. Palmer open Isleworth. Shortly thereafter we exchanged wedding vows. Life was exciting! The following year we were off to Australia, as Brad seized upon a remarkable opportunity to be a part of bringing the Arnold Palmer name to Sanctuary Cove.

I still had not yet met this man my husband affectionately referred to as "the King," but I can assure you, for this newlywed who was vying to be Brad's "queen," Mr. Palmer was definitely competition for me! We settled in, set up shop, and got to work.

In January 1988, Sanctuary Cove launched a weeklong, multi-million-dollar opening extravaganza. One of the events was a star-studded golf tournament, with an unprecedented million-dollar winner's check. I was thrilled with the opportunity to participate. The threesome I was following that day consisted of Brad; Ian Baker-Finch, Sanctuary Cove's resident touring pro; and the King, Arnold Palmer.

We were on the first tee and Mr. Palmer had just been formally announced, to great fanfare and applause. I knew very little about golf back then, but having played tennis as a professional amateur, I at least knew the two sports shared some of the same courtesies. As we all watched, Mr. Palmer began to set up behind his ball and proceeded to go through his pre-shot routine. This includes a tug on his glove and a slight adjustment to his visor. He placed his driver next to his teed-up ball and began his takeaway, swinging his driver back for the shot, when an elderly woman called out from behind the ropes in her most polite Aussie accent, "Mr. Palmer! Oh, Mr. Palmer! May I have your autograph, please?"

People gasped, heads turned, and I thought, *Oh, you are such dead meat, woman. Even I know better than to do that!* At that point, I expected the King to give her "the look" or perhaps "the talk." We've all seen clips of hot-headed athletes who quickly melt down if someone dares break their concentration.

But Arnie did no such thing. Instead, he stopped mid-swing, handed his driver to his caddie, calmly removed his glove and visor, and made his way to the ropes. He asked her for her name and then asked how she was doing on this fine day. He gave her an autograph and thanked her. He thanked her!

I will never forget the lesson I learned that day. In my heart, Arnold Palmer is the "King of golf" because he remains grateful to those who put him on his throne.

In closing, I'd like to share one more anecdote related to just how strongly Arnie feels about treating the fans with respect and gratitude. My friends Dicky Pride and Peter Jacobsen are both PGA Tour professionals and all-around good guys. Well, each of these fellows at one time had signed an illegible autograph in the presence of the King. Arnold Palmer, acting like a father to these "sons," took it upon himself to remind them that a legible signature is a sign of a sincere gratitude attitude. Here's Peter's account of an early autograph session with Arnie.

THE ART OF AUTOGRAPHS
Peter Jacobsen

It was early in my career and Arnold and I had just finished an exhibition event in Los Angeles. We were signing autographs prior to heading into the locker room, and as I was finishing my signature on a visor for a young boy, Arnold looked over at me and said, "What is that?"

I looked up to see his eyes affixed on the scribble that I just put on a perfectly good visor. There was my childhood idol looking at me like I just scratched his new Cadillac. Before I could even make sense of what he was referring to or, better yet, answer, Arnold said, "You know, these people are worthy of being able to read who it was that signed their memento. You should respect that enough to take your time and sign your name where people can actually read it."

I never forgot that moment, and Arnold's comments resonated with me. I do my best to sign an autograph to be proud of, and I have also called out some of my younger playing partners the very same way that Arnold did for me. I feel, along with Mr. Palmer, that this is one of the simplest gestures that makes a huge difference in our sport and the future success of it. It's about the gratification and appreciation of those who support us each and every week on the Tour. Without them, we wouldn't be living the dream!

While very few of us are asked to give autographs, each one of us owes those in our circle of influence respect and gratitude. Life has a way of swinging on the hinges of very small things. When you're talking with someone, whether it's your spouse, child, or colleague, are you looking them in the eye—or looking over their shoulder? Do you look for opportunities to let those close to you know how much you love them by sending a card, a note, or some flowers? You should never underestimate the potentially large impact of a seemingly small act.

I would encourage you to live the Arnold Palmer way—always grateful.

Mind Your Manners

IS THERE ANY OTHER sport where a competitor will call a penalty on himself? In what other game will you find archrivals wishing each other good luck at the beginning of a match or calling out "Nice shot" during the heat of battle? Golfers are a unique group of people who relish the integrity and honor of honesty and fair play. For the vast majority of players, respecting and maintaining the traditions of the game are more important than claiming victory.

And who better epitomizes all that is good and noble about the game of golf than Arnold Palmer? With his permission, I would like to share some thoughts on this topic straight from his memoirs, *A Golfer's Life*:[1]

> The truth is when I see modern stars of the game ignoring the basic fundamentals of personal courtesy or worse, treating fans and even sponsors with indifference or disrespect, suggesting they simply feel entitled to the enormous amounts of money, opportunity, and social prestige the game brings their way, I worry about the future of golf, because it means something vital is no longer being given back to the game and those who support it. It saddens me to no end when I realize many younger players don't know the history of the game that gives them such rich and splendid lives, possess little appreciation of how and why the profes-

sional game has grown the way it has in the past fifty years, and have no apparent interest in understanding the important traditions of the game and perpetuating them. Ours is a game — and for that matter, ours is a nation — of such simple abundance I sometimes feel it's downright criminal to take the many ordinary blessings we enjoy for granted. It's my belief that we do so at our own peril.

Life be not so short but that there is always time for courtesy.
RALPH WALDO EMERSON

Believe me, as someone who had a hand in creating the concept of sports marketing, I'm all for athletes getting handsomely paid for what they are worth, but nobody is above the rules, etiquette, and traditions of the game.

As I've gotten older, I've realized that we need to be constantly challenged to examine ourselves and see what we can give back to this life. Several years ago, for instance, my friend and neighbor Dr. Tom Moran, former chief of surgery at Latrobe Hospital, challenged me to come up with a way to assist the hospital where I was born. The hospital was in the midst of a critical expansion of much-needed services and facilities. What I proposed and carried out, with the help of a few insiders, especially my sister Cheech, and the support of many generous people in western Pennsylvania and elsewhere, was an event we dubbed our "golf gala."

We created a one-day affair with a four-man skins game along with a lavish dinner and amateur scramble. All I had to do, it seemed, was ask my Tour buddies, several of the top players, and they said they would be happy to help out. We did this for six years running, alternating between Latrobe and Laurel Valley, and cleared more than $3.5 million for the hospital, putting it in the hands of a newly formed foundation headed by Dr. Bob Mazero.

To give you an idea of why we had no trouble drawing a crowd for the skins game, here's who we had each year: 1992 — Curtis Strange, Chi Chi Rodriguez, and Dow Finsterwald; 1993 — Greg Norman, Dave Marr, and Rocco Mediate; 1994 — Jack Nicklaus, Jay Haas, and Peter Jacobsen; 1995 — Lee Trevino, Gary Player, and Fuzzy Zoeller; 1996 — Nick Price, Raymond Floyd, and Fred Couples; and 1997 — Tiger Woods, Tom Lehman, and Davis Love III. They not only came as a favor to me but, under the most gentle of prodding, turned their winnings over to the hospital as well.

That's how professional golf gives back to the lives of people, and I'm very proud to be a caretaker or an ambassador in that process.

I have been associated with and worked for quite a few other charitable organizations and causes over the years, the most extensive connection being with another charity that focuses on children in need. That was my twenty-year tenure as Honorary National Chairman of the March of Dimes Birth Defects Foundation. I still get emotional when I look at campaign promotional photos taken with bright, brave youngsters each year back in the 1970s and 1980s who, I know from letters I receive, have gone on to have successful and productive lives. I'm pleased to have made whatever contribution I made, and it was great to work with such devoted March of Dimes people.

As previously mentioned, Arnold Palmer has taken his responsibilities as one of golf's elder statesmen seriously. But there is a reason why Arnie's Army has followed him, literally and figuratively, over the years. It wasn't just the success and the wins on the big tour. There were plenty of other successful golfers to follow and stars to chase. Nor was it the lure of fame or fortune. Nearly all in Arnie's Army were nameless, anonymous faces in the crowd.

So what was it? What was behind the devotion of the King's fans?

I think people loved Arnie because Arnie loved them. He was also one of them — flawed and faulted, impetuous and impatient. He wore his emotions on his sleeve. He had guts. He took risks. He wasn't afraid to fail. He also had a sense of humor. And he did it all with a sense of style and class. He was a gentleman, a golfer who held firm to the belief that chivalry never goes out of style.

Cherish the Time You Have

AS HE ENTERS HIS ninth decade of life, Arnold Palmer is keenly aware just how quickly the days and years have gone. Somebody once said that youth is wasted on the young, but to scan the timeline of the King's career, you'd get the sense Palmer has made very good use of his time.

Time has always been a precious commodity to Arnold Palmer. In fact, if you visit Arnold Palmer's website, you'll find the following statement: "Palmer and Rolex. Masters of style. Standards of excellence. Rolex has shared every second of Arnold Palmer's life for the last 34 years."[1]

When it comes to endorsing products, the King is both incredibly discerning (i.e., picky) and fiercely loyal (i.e., he has many long-standing sponsor relationships). As you're well aware, Rolex crafts one of the finest timepieces in the world. Quality usually comes with a price, and the typical Rolex watch runs in the thousands of dollars. I'll admit that there was a time when I assumed people who purchased the brand were merely chasing a status symbol. Although many undoubtedly do just that, I remember overhearing an exchange between Arnie and his manager, Alistair Johnston, which provided me with a new perspective.

"Allie," Arnold said, "it's not about the money, it's about the time. Because my time is the most valuable thing I have."

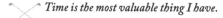 *Time is the most valuable thing I have.*

ARNOLD PALMER

Over the years I saved my pennies, and now my own Rolex reminds me of Mr. Palmer's words of wisdom. Whenever I glance down at my wrist, I'm reminded to value not only my time but also the time of others. The stewardship of our resources is important, but those resources will serve only those who have the time to use them to serve others.

CELEBRATING A LIFE WELL LIVED

Back in September of 2009, my wife, Wanda, and I were invited to attend a magnificent party celebrating both Arnold Palmer's eightieth birthday and the twentieth anniversary celebration for the Arnold Palmer Medical Center for Women and Children. It was a star-studded evening from beginning to end. There were warm video greetings from three United States presidents and dozens upon dozens of celebrities, athletes, and fellow professional golfers. Amy Grant and Vince Gill led those gathered in singing "Happy Birthday," followed by a private concert. It was a celebration befitting the King. The culmination of the evening came when Mr. Palmer greeted the guests and expressed his appreciation for the festivities. It was classic Palmer—a perfect mix of humor and poignant sentiment—and when he finished, there wasn't a dry eye in the house.

LAUDED BY HIS PEERS

The highest compliment a man can enjoy usually comes from the lips of his peers. These are the people who know what you do, do what you do, and see what you do. There are very few secrets inside the PGA Tour; fellow golfers see how you act behind closed doors in the clubhouse, in the parking lots, and on the planes when the cameras are off. And so, given on the occasion of Arnie's eightieth birthday, these tributes from Palmer's friends and fellow competitors really sum up the lesson of cherishing the time they've had with a man who has cherished the time he's been given here on earth.[2]

Mr. Palmer is now in his twilight, with more years behind than ahead. It's been a wildly successful and exciting journey. In the following tributes, the many decades of living have been boiled down to a precious few words. As you read these warm sentiments, you might consider how your family will remember *you*. What will be said? What will be forgotten? The good news is that there is still time to impact the final word.

Rocco Mediate: "Arnold Palmer is timeless, that's all there is to it."

Tom Watson: "Frank Beard said that we owe eighty cents of every dollar we earn to Arnold. That's true."

Jack Nicklaus: "Arnold brought a lot more to the game than just his game. What I mean by that is there's no question about his record and his ability to play the game. He was very, very good at that. But he obviously brought a lot more. He was there at the right time with television, and his flair and his charisma were things that were really very, very important to the game of golf at that time."

Davis Love III: "Arnold has always been a leader who stood out from the rest, and for a lot of different reasons. He always said the right thing, did the right thing. He is as solid a human being as you could ever find in any walk of life."

Ben Crenshaw: "I met Arnold in 1970. He was playing in the PGA at Southern Hills CC that year. He came to the Texas Open Junior tournament at Wichita Falls CC to give an exhibition, and I played nine holes with him and two others. He just couldn't have been nicer. I was eighteen, and I was just in awe of him. Made an impression on me, though, too because he was just so genuine. He understood what an impact he could have on younger people, and he took that responsibility and set an example."

Jim Furyk: "You can always go back in time—Bobby Jones, Byron Nelson, Sam Snead, Ben Hogan—and go through great upon great, but I think he was the pioneer. Tiger might have made golf cooler, but Arnold was probably the first cool golfer—a good-looking guy, the shirtsleeves showing the big arms, go for broke. Everyone rooted for him. I think that our sport would be a lot different and look a lot different without him."

Nick Price: "I met him at Muirfield at the British Open in 1980. He walked past me, and I said, 'Hi, Mr. Palmer,' kind of sheepishly. I got to really know him later when I lived in Orlando. You build someone up in your mind to be bigger than life, and I'm sure this happens a lot where maybe you get disappointed once you get to know them. That wasn't the case with Arnold. I mean, he was bigger than life, and yet he was just this very personable guy who you could really talk to."

Fred Couples: "First time I met Arnold was in Portland at Peter Jacobsen's tournament, and that was something special because ever since, he's basically been like another father figure in a way. You have a chance to talk with him, and he gives you so much. He's asking you questions—how's your game, how are you doing? He's like your grandfather, really. That's almost how I look at him. There isn't a time when I see him that I don't give him a kiss on the cheek. That's how I feel about him, and I know that a lot of other guys sort of feel the same way, that you love him like he's your father or grandfather. I love all the old guys, Jack, Ray Floyd, [Lee] Trevino. But would any of them say that Arnold wasn't the most special of them all? I don't think so."

Each and every one of these individuals has cherished his time with Arnold Palmer, and, to a man, each would tell you that his time with the King has gone too fast. I would add my voice to theirs; all too often we fail to notice or appreciate our blessings until they're gone. I have dedicated the last twenty-five years of my life to working alongside Arnold Palmer. Next to being a husband, father, and son, it has been the highlight of my life. My friend and hero is a man now in the twilight of his career, but how I love that he still tackles every project with the same passion and demand for excellence.

> *Dost thou love life? Then do not squander time, for that is the stuff life is made of.*
>
> BENJAMIN FRANKLIN

It's popular to lament the shortage of heroes today, but those who do would be wise to keep looking. It's true you might have to look longer or harder, but they are there. You've been reading about one such man, imperfect and faulted, but a remarkable man of our time all the same. How fortunate we have been to live in an era of so many terrific and upstanding giants of golf. The sun is now setting on their time and season, and others are struggling to assume their place in the sun. But please allow me to be blunt and perfectly clear: somebody might take Arnold's title as the "King" someday, but nobody will ever take his place.

Arnold Palmer has clearly appreciated and cherished the time he's been given. He has long understood that true joy is found not in receiving, but in the joyful act of giving. He's taught me many, many things, but none more important than this: it is only when I joyfully give of myself that I will fully tap into the abundance of everything I really need.

That is all. That is enough.

The Caretaker

Arnold Palmer

I'LL LET YOU IN on a little secret, something I've admitted to only a handful of folks. I never cared for the nickname "the King." At times, it makes me uncomfortable and even a bit irritated to be referred to that way. There is no king of golf. Never has been, never will be. Golf is the most democratic game on earth, a pastime of the people that grants no special privileges and pays no mind to whether a man is a hotel doorman or a corporate CEO. It punishes and exalts us all with splendid equal opportunity.

I'm the son of a hard-nosed caretaker who had large hands and an even larger heart, but a man who drilled into me the importance of always leaving the golf course better than I found it. I feel we have to be more vigilant than ever to make certain the things that make golf such a great game remain the same and are protected and nurtured and preserved for the next people coming along.

I do like being seen as and called an ambassador of the game. It is a role I take very seriously in my work with the USGA [United States Golf Association] and whenever I am in the public eye. But I suppose at the end of the day what I really am, inescapably — and I prefer to be thought of in terms of my legacy — is a caretaker of the game just the way my father was before me.

ACKNOWLEDGMENTS

I THANK GOD FOR the many blessings in my life. I am the product of the many lives that have touched mine, many of whom helped me channel the courage to tackle the dream of writing and producing this book. This long list includes my dad, Paul Brewer, Arnold Palmer, Doc Giffen, Wanda Brewer, Robert Wolgemuth, Erik Wolgemuth, Jack Nicklaus, Michael Jordan, Ivan Lendl, Ian Baker-Finch, Dicky Pride, Peter Jacobsen, Bob Proctor, Beth Pry, Ted Purdy, Mitch Burke, Gary Lorfano, Howdy Giles, and the entire group at Zondervan. A very special gratitude to Paul Batura, who so eloquently and skillfully transformed my stories into literature. Paul, you are a true artist and I am humbled by your great work and walk in faith with the Lord.

The unconditional love exhibited and taught to me by my mother, Rita Claire Brewer, and her unique way of always seeing the good in everyone and everything conditioned my eyes and ears and heart to see, hear, and feel the goodness in other people. She was also my inspiration to write, and I know that her spirit has been with me every step of the way, gleaming with joy from heaven above.

PASS IT ON

Our charity of choice is the Arnold Palmer Medical Center. I am so grateful for everything they do to help women and children battle so many difficult health issues. Please join me in continuing to pray for their healing. I give thanks to all who have purchased this book, knowing that a percentage of the proceeds will support this worthy need. You can learn more about APMC by visiting *www.orlandohealth.com/arnoldpalmerhospital.*

NOTES

PREFACE: ON THE TEE BOX WITH ARNOLD PALMER

1. Anthony Gross, *Lincoln's Own Stories* (New York: Harper & Brothers, 1912; repr., East Sussex, UK: Gardners, 2007).
2. Gerry Dulac, "Arnie Didn't Play Today's Head Games," *Pittsburgh Post-Gazette*, April 13, 2003, C5.
3. Personal interview with Arnold Palmer.

PART 1
Life-Changing Lessons Are Often "Deceptively Simple"

LESSON 1: REMEMBER YOUR ROOTS

1. *Arnold Palmer*: www.arnoldpalmer.com/ALLARNIE/biography3.aspx.
2. Dulac, "Arnie Didn't Play Today's Head Games."
3. Ibid.
4. *MotivateUs.com*: www.motivateus.com/rememb-8.htm.
5. Gerry Dulac, "Q&A with Arnold Palmer," Scripps Howard News Service, July 4, 2005.

LESSON 2: YOU ARE WHAT YOU THINK

1. This poem has been referenced as "Thinker" or "The Victor" and erroneously attributed to Napoleon Hill, C. W. Longenecker, and Henry Ford.
2. Kevin Childs, "A Record Field in the Race for Wills," *The Age*, March 21, 1992.
3. Personal interview with Arnold Palmer.
4. Graeme Lennox, "Lawn Tennis: Andy's In with a Shout; Teen Star Still Needs Mental Workout, Says Mind Guru; So You Want to Be a Shrink," *Sunday Mail* (Glasgow, Scotland), July 2, 2006, 1.
5. Yogi Berra, *Things People Said*: www.rinkworks.com/said/yogiberra.shtml/.

6. Fulton J. Sheen.

7. Arthur Gordon, "Lenten Guideposts," *Vidella-Messenger* (UK), April 6, 1957, 8.

8. Paul Harvey, "A Message of Freedom with Responsibility," Landon Lecture Series, September 19, 2003.

9. Chris Cobbs, "Put a Swing on DVD," *Orlando Sentinel*, March 27, 2002.

10. Fulton J. Sheen, *Life Is Worth Living* (Fort Collins, Colo.: Ignatius Press, 1999), 15.

11. *Billy Graham, Norman Vincent Peale, Archbishop Fulton Sheen, Robert Schuller, The Four Greatest Inspirational Speakers and Preachers of the 20th Century* (Garden Grove, Calif: Crystal Cathedral Ministries, 1997).

LESSON 3: TELL ME THAT I AM READY

1. Gordon Monson, "Swagger and Other Jazz," *Salt Lake Tribune*, March 25, 1997.

2. Muhammad Ali, *Inner Treasures*: *www.kaleidosoul.com/support-files /innertreasures.pdf*.

3. Muhammad Ali, *Brainy Quote*: *www.brainyquote.com/quotes /authors/m/muhammad_ali_2.html*.

4. Michael Sandrock, "Juma Ikangaa," *Running with the Legends: Training and Racing Insights from 21 Great Runners* (Champaign, Ill.: Human Kinetics, 1996), 403–20.

5. For more information, see *www.pgatour.com/qschool/*.

6. Kenneth H. Blanchard and Spencer Johnson, *The One Minute Manager* (New York: William Morrow, 1982).

7. Tom Rath, *StrengthsFinder 2.0* (New York: Gallup Press, 2007).

8. *Friday Study Ministries*: *www.fridaystudy.org/html/genesis /genesis37_19_20.htm*.

9. James E. Loehr, *The New Toughness Training for Sports: Mental, Emotional, and Physical Conditioning from One of the World's Premier Sports Psychologists* (New York: Dutton, 1994).

10. Wayde Goodall, *Success Kills: Sidestep the Snares That Will Steal Your Dreams* (Green Forest, Ariz.: New Leaf, 2009), 39.

LESSON 4: SIMPLIFY THE COMPLEX

1. Raul Dominguez, "Maddening, Rewarding: Golf Greatest Game Ever," *San Antonio Express-News*, April 9, 2000, 2L; Bill Kirby, "Golf Tugs at Heart, Pocketbook," *Augusta Chronicle*, April 6, 1997, A11.
2. Phillippa Lally, Cornelia H. M. van Jaarsveld, Henry W. W. Potts, and Jane Wardle, "How Are Habits Formed: Modelling Habit Formation in the Real World," *European Journal of Social Psychology*, July 2009.
3. Paul Franklin, "Golf Legend Arnold Palmer Honored at USGA Museum," *Home News Tribune* (N.J.), June 3, 2008.
4. Ibid.
5. *Baseball Almanac*: *www.baseball-almanac.com/quotes/quopaig.shtml*.

LESSON 5: DEFINE YOUR WORTHY IDEAL

1. To our best knowledge, this quote has never been officially attributed to any individual.
2. Muhammad Ali, *ThinkExist*: http://thinkexist.com/quotation /champions_aren-t_made_in_the_gyms-champions_are/289453. html.
3. Andrew Carnegie.
4. Robert I. Fitzhenry, *The Harper Book of Quotations* (New York: HarperCollins, 2005), 431.
5. George Harrison, "Any Road," *Brainwashed* (Dark Horse/EMI, 2002).
6. John M. Ross, "Palmer on Palmer's Future," *Golf*, February 1972.
7. Ibid.

LESSON 6: ALWAYS GIVE A FIRM HANDSHAKE

1. Jerry Tarde, "A Tale of Two Kings," *Golf Digest*, October 2008, 18.
2. Damon Hack, "McCormack and Palmer Changed the World of Sports and Business Forever," *Golf*, December 16, 2008.
3. *IMG*: *www.imgworld.com/home/default.sps*.
4. Paul J. Zak, "The Power of a Handshake: How Touch Sustains Personal and Business Relationships," *Huffington Post*: *www. HuffingtonPost.com*, September 28, 2008.

5. Ibid.

6. Personal correspondence with Dicky Pride.

7. Proverbs 10:4 KJV.

LESSON 7: LEAVE THE WORLD BETTER THAN YOU FOUND IT

1. The first version of the Shootout was played with just the one foursome — Greg Norman, Arnold Palmer, Jack Nicklaus, and Raymond Floyd — as a fundraiser for what is now the Arnold Palmer Medical Center in Orlando. For more information, see *www.thesharkshootout.com/news_121108.php*.

2. If you want to read of a man who takes calculated risks and exemplifies the many wonderful lessons of Arnold Palmer, I would encourage you to read the story of Harris Rosen. Mr. Rosen has been president of Rosen Hotels and Resorts since 1974, after leaving a comfortable position with the Walt Disney Company to pursue his dream of owning and operating his own hotel. The public service announcement was titled "Keep America Beautiful," *YouTube*: *www.youtube.com/watch?v=m4ozVMxzNAA*.

3. Keep America Beautiful, *Wikipedia*: *http://en.wikipedia.org/wiki /Keep_America_Beautiful*.

4. For a more complete listing and for contact information, see *Arnold Palmer*: *www.arnoldpalmer.com/ALLARNIE/charities.aspx*.

LESSON 8: ALWAYS PLAY FOR THE LOVE OF THE GAME

1. Bob Hope and Dwayne Netland, *Bob Hope's Confessions of a Hooker: My Lifelong Affair with Golf* (New York: Doubleday, 1985).

2. Ibid.

3. Ibid.

4. George Sheehan, *Dr. Sheehan on Running* (Mountain Views, Calif.: World, 1975).

5. "December 22, 1849: Dostoevsky Reprieved at Last Minute," *History*: *www.history.com/this-day-in-history/dostoevsky-reprieved-at -last-minute*.

6. Fyodor Dostoevsky, *Crime and Punishment* (New York: Modern Library, 1950).

7. Fyodor Dostoevsky, *The Possessed* (New York: Modern Library, 1936).

8. Fyodor Dostoevsky, *The Brothers Karamazov* (Chicago: University of Chicago Press, 1971).

9. Charles W. Colson and Harold Fickett, *The Good Life* (Wheaton, Ill.: Tyndale, 2005).

10. George Sheehan, *Running and Being: The Total Experience* (Kernersville, N.C.: Second Wind, 1998).

11. Sheehan, *Dr. Sheehan on Running*.

LESSON 9: GET THE BALL TO THE HOLE

1. "Golf Quotes," *Gold Coast Bulletin*, December 14, 2006, 91.

2. Edwin H. Friedman, *A Failure of Nerve: Leadership in the Age of the Quick Fix* (New York: Seabury, 2007).

LESSON 10: YOU GET OUT OF IT WHAT YOU PUT INTO IT

1. *Yahoo! Sports*: *http://sports.yahoo.com/golf/pga/leaderboard/1994/25*.

2. *National Post*: *http://nationalpost.stats.com/golf/golfer .asp?tour=PGA&golfer=0138*.

3. *Famous Quotes & Authors*: *www.famousquotesandauthors.com/keywords /melons_quotes.html*.

PART 2
Your Starting Point Influences Your Destination

1. J. F. Kennedy, Address June 25 in *Public Papers of the Presidents of United States* (Washington, D.C.: Office of the Federal Register, 1964), 519.

LESSON 11: TAP INTO THE POWER OF IMAGINATION

1. *A Christmas Story* (Hollywood: MGM/UA, 1983) was first released in theaters in 1983.

2. Ibid.

3. *Rudy* (Hollywood: TriStar, 1993) was first released in theaters on October 13, 1993.

4. *Rudy International*: *www.rudyint.com/truestory.cfm*.

5. *Rudy* (TriStar, 1993).
6. Ibid.
7. *Quote DB*: *www.quotedb.com/quotes/3143*.
8. Mental imagery, also called "visualization and mental rehearsal," is defined as experience that resembles perceptual experience, but which occurs in the absence of the appropriate stimuli for the relevant perception (*http://plato.stanford.edu/entries/mental-imagery/*). Whenever we imagine ourselves performing an action in the absence of physical practice, we are said to be using imagery. While most discussions of imagery focus on the visual mode, there exist other modes of experience such as auditory and kinesthetic that are just as important. See *www.vanderbilt.edu/AnS/psychology/health_psychology/mentalimagery.html*.
9. Jack Nicklaus, "Mental Imagery," *BrianMac Sports Coach*: *www.brianmac.co.uk/mental.htm*.
10. *Nicklaus*: *www.nicklaus.com/nicklaus_facts/pgatour.php*.
11. *The Wire*: *www.golfbusinesswire.com/releases/119988*.

LESSON 12: DEVELOPING THE MASTER'S TOUCH

1. Richard Southern, *The Making of the Middle Ages* (New Haven, Conn.: Yale University Press, 1953; repr., Fredericksburg, Va.: BookCrafters, 1992), Ch.IV(II.B).
2. Ian O'Connor, *Arnie and Jack: Palmer, Nicklaus, and Golf's Greatest Rivalry* (Boston: Houghton Mifflin, 2008), 211.
3. Ibid.
4. Bobby Jones, *Rights and Wrongs of Golf* (New York: A. G. Spalding, 1935).
5. Byron Nelson, *Winning Golf* (London: MacDonald, 1947).
6. Doug Ferguson, "A Different Age in Golf: Nicklaus Sees Many Changes, and Not All for the Good," *Charleston Gazette*, May 28, 2008, 4B.

LESSON 13: PLAN TO WIN

1. Gary Player, a native of South Africa, famously beat Arnold Palmer in the 1961 Masters by one stroke. Player also won the famed tournament in 1974 and 1978.

2. *Golf Digest*: *www.golfdigest.com/golf-courses/golf-courses /2009-05/100_greatestgolfcourses*.

3. For a full list of archived results, see *www.masters.com*.

LESSON 14: TRUST BUT VERIFY

1. Ronald Reagan, "Farewell Address to the Nation," January 11, 1989, *Ronald Reagan*: *www.ronaldreagan.com/sp_21.html*.

2. Tom Shales, "The Pageant on a Day of Grace," *Washington Post*, December 9, 1987, B1.

3. Martin Lader, United Press International, November 15, 1984.

4. *Monterey County*: *http://montereysearch.com/*.

5. *Golf Today*: *www.golftoday.co.uk/news/yeartodate/news99/pebble.html*.

LESSON 15: DARE TO CARE

1. For a full list of results, see *http://sports.yahoo.com/golf/pga /leaderboard/1991/29*.

2. For more information on the history of St. Andrews, see *www. worldgolf.com/courses/world/the-old-course.htm*.

3. Matthew L. Wald, "Golf: Pro Golfer and Five Others Die in a Baffling Jet Accident," *New York Times*, October 26, 1999, A1.

4. Michael Mayo, "Payne's Priorities Were in Order," *Sun-Sentinel* (Fort Lauderdale, Fla.), October 26, 1999, 1C.

LESSON 16: THE BEST ATTRACT THE BEST

1. To view a clip of the original Gatorade commercial, visit *YouTube*: *www.youtube.com/watch?v=b0AGiq9j_Ak*.

2. Ibid.

3. *PGA Tour*: *www.pgatour.com/players/01/98/81/*.

4. The Golf Channel is the new home for Shell's Wonderful World of Golf series, a time-honored golf tradition that features one-on-one matches between some of golf's biggest superstars. Broadcast veteran Jack Whitaker will serve as host, with Judy Rankin and Jennifer Biehn reporting from the course. See *www.thegolfchannel. com/core.aspx?page=23614*.

5. *Basketball-Reference.com*: *www.basketball-reference.com/allstar /NBA_1992.html*.

6. *NBA*: *www.nba.com/allstar2007/1992_allstar.html*.
7. "Air's Army: Jordan Plays with Palmer in Pro-Am, Holding His Own and Drawing 17,500," Associated Press, July 16, 1993.
8. Ibid.
9. Michael Jordan, "Fear Is an illusion," November 5, 2006, *Empowered By Excellence!*: *http://aidysteveany.myaiesec.net/2006/11/fear-is-illusion.html*.

PART 3
Optimism Rules the Kingdom

1. Friedrich Nietzsche, *The Twilight of the Idols, or How to Philosophise with the Hammer* (Edinburgh: T. N. Foulis, 1919).
2. Arnold Palmer with James Dodson, *A Golfer's Life* (New York: Random House, 1999).

LESSON 17: GO FOR BROKE

1. Arnold Palmer with William Barry Furlong, *Go for Broke: My Philosophy of Winning Golf* (New York: Simon & Schuster, 1973).
2. Ibid., 252.
3. John Paul Newport, "Palmer's Go-for-It Greatness," *Wall Street Journal*, September 11, 2009.
4. *Golf Legends*: *www.golflegends.org/us-open.php*.
5. Newport, "Palmer's Go-for-It Greatness."
6. For biographical information on Dr. Norman Vincent Peale, see *www.marblechurch.org/Default.aspx?tabid=91*.
7. Norman Vincent Peale, *You Can If You Think You Can* (Englewood Cliffs, N.J.: Prentice Hall, 1974), 246; Basil King, *The Conquest of Fear* (New York: Doubleday, 1948).
8. Newport, "Palmer's Go-for-It Greatness."
9. *National Golf Foundation*: *www.ngf.org*.

LESSON 18: USE FEAR FOR FUEL

1. J. R. R. Tolkien, *World of Quotes*: *www.worldofquotes.com/topic/Fear/index.html*.
2. Arnold D. Palmer, *The Turning Point: The 54th Amateur Champi-*

enship of the United States Golf Association 1954. Winner: Arnold D. Palmer* (Ooltewah, Tenn.: ProGroup, 1983).
3. Robert Collier.

LESSON 19: THE POWER OF PERSEVERANCE

1. For more information, see *www.tpc.com*.
2. Di Freeze, "Arnold Palmer and His Pilots — A Close-Knit Fraternity," *Airport Journal*, November 2004.
3. Woody Allen, *The Quotations Page*: *www.quotationspage.com/quotes /Woody_Allen*.

LESSON 20: TURN ADVERSITY TO YOUR ADVANTAGE

1. Jeff Babineau, "Palmer Begins His Fight Today; Golf: Arnold Palmer Diagnosed with Prostate Cancer," *Orlando Sentinel*, January 13, 1997, C9.
2. George Sweda, "Palmer Takes Aggressive Action," *Cleveland Plain Dealer*, January 25, 1997, 5D.
3. *Prostate Cancer Foundation*: *www.prostatecancerfoundation.org/site /c.itIWK2OSG/b.49886/k.815/Arnies_Army.htm*.
4. *Urological Sciences Research Foundation*: *www.usrf.org/news /010815-Arnold_Palmer_CaP.html*.
5. The history of Arnold Palmer as related by Arnold Palmer and Chris Byrd, founding partner of Arnold Palmer Tee: Mr. Palmer had been privately brewing a mixture of lemonade and iced tea in his home for many years. In the late 1960s, in a bar in Palm Springs, California, Mr. Palmer ordered a mixture of lemonade and iced tea, and a woman seated next to him overheard his order and said, "I'll have that Palmer drink." The drink then spread across the golfing world and became known as an "Arnold Palmer."

LESSON 21: COMPLIMENT AND ENCOURAGE

1. *Peter Jacobsen Golf*: *http://peterjacobsengolf.com/careertimeline.htm*.
2. *Peter Jacobsen Golf*: *http://peterjacobsengolf.com/music.htm*.
3. New lyrics by Peter Jacobsen, based on "Smuggler's Blues" by Glenn Frey. "Smuggler's Blues" words and music by Glenn Frey and Jack Tempchin.

4. Peter Jacobsen and Jack Sheehan, *Embedded Balls: Adventures On and Off the Tour with Golf's Premier Storyteller* (New York: G. P. Putnam's Sons, 2005).

5. Peter Jacobsen, *Buried Lies: True Tales and Tall Stories from the PGA Tour* (New York: G. P. Putnam's Sons, 1993).

LESSON 22: BELIEVE IN YOURSELF

1. "Palmer to Receive Congressional Gold Medal," Associated Press, October 3, 2009.

2. Ibid.

PART 4
Heroes in Action

1. W. Flemon McIntosh Jr., "Come, Let Us Reason Together: What is the purpose of your life?" *News Herald* (Morganton, N.C.), *Visit Burke County*: *www.visitburkecounty.com/reasontogether.html*.

2. "Edison Sees His Vast Plant Burn," *New York Times*, December 10, 1914, A1.

3. McIntosh, "Come, Let Us Reason Together."

LESSON 23: TURN NEGATIVES INTO POSITIVES

1. Norman Vincent Peale, "What to Do about Difficulties," *Positive Thinking Bible* (Nashville: Thomas Nelson, 1998), 1128 (the words of Jesus are from Matthew 21:21–22).

2. J. R. R. Tolkien, *The Hobbit* (Boston: Houghton Mifflin Harcourt, 2007).

3. J. R. R. Tolkien, *The Lord of the Rings* (Boston: Houghton Mifflin, 2005).

4. *Eucatastrophe*: *www.eucatastrophe.com/blog/archives/category/tolkien-tuesdays/*.

5. Kemmons Wilson and Robert Kerr, *Half Luck, Half Brains: The Kemmons Wilson Holiday Inn Story* (Nashville: Hambleton Hill, 1996).

6. Ibid.; *InterContinental Hotels Group*: *www.ichotelsgroup.com/*.

7. Adrian Rogers, *Adrianisms: The Wit and Wisdom of Adrian Rogers* (Memphis: Love Worth Finding Ministries, 2006).

LESSON 24: PRESSURE PRODUCES RESULTS

1. "History of U.S. Steel," *U.S. Steel*: *www.ussteel.com/corp/company /profile/history.asp*.
2. *Brazilian Football Academy*: *www.icfds.com/*.
3. Daniel Coyle, *The Talent Code: Greatness Isn't Born. It's Grown. Here's How* (New York: Bantam, 2009).
4. Wayne Dyer, *Your Erroneous Zones* (New York: HarperCollins, 1993), 31.

LESSON 25: GETTING INTO THE ZONE

1. Bob Proctor, *The Secret* documentary (2006), *PR.com*: *www.pr.com /article/1064*.
2. Jeanie Lerche Davis, "Athletes in the Zone: They're Not Neurotic," *WebMD Health News*: *www.webmd.com/news/*, August 13, 2004.
3. Norman Vincent Peale, *The Power of Positive Thinking* (New York: Fireside, 2003), 52.
4. *Institute of HeartMath*: *www.heartmath.com*.
5. You can learn more about HeartMath through my website, *www. bradbrewer.com*.

LESSON 27: BELIEVE IN A DREAM

1. Richard Sandomir, "TV Sports: For Hard-Core Fans, New Channel Offers All Golf, All the Time," *New York Times*, January 13, 1995, B13.
2. Ibid.

LESSON 29: CAPITALIZE ON YOUR SUCCESS

1. *Tennis Corner*: *www.tenniscorner.net/index.php?corner=m&action =players&playerid=LEI001*.
2. Pat Williams and Michael Weinreb, *How to Be Like Mike: Life Lessons about Basketball's Best* (Deerfield Beach, Fla.: Health Communications, 2001).

PART 5
A True Champion's Attitude Is Gratitude

LESSON 30: DON'T DWELL ON YESTERDAY'S NEWS
1. James C. Dobson recalling the Pasadena College tennis trophy. Used with permission.

LESSON 31: BEFRIEND YOUR ENEMIES
1. George Peper, "Golf Magazine Interview: Arnold Palmer and Jack Nicklaus," May 1994, *Golf*: *www.golf.com/golf/advertisers/dow /humanside/profiles/a_palmer_j_nicklaus.htm*, July 11, 2009.
2. Ibid.

LESSON 32: RESPECT FOR EVERY MAN
1. Doug Ferguson, "A Chance Meeting with the King That Gore Won't Forget," Associated Press, March 27, 2009.
2. Ibid.
3. *PGA Tour*: *www.pgatour.com/players/02/28/92/*.
4. Ibid.

LESSON 34: MIND YOUR MANNERS
1. Arnold Palmer with James Dodson, *A Golfer's Life* (New York: Random House, 1999).

LESSON 35: CHERISH THE TIME YOU HAVE
1. *Arnold Palmer*: *www.arnoldpalmer.com/brands/endorsements.aspx*.
2. Dave Shedloski and Jerry Cooke, "What He Means to Me," *Golf World*, September 14, 2009, 16.